A Neuropsychologist's Guide to Training Psychometrists

A Neuropsychologist's Guide to Training Psychometrists: Promoting Competence in Psychological Testing provides a framework for busy neuropsychologists faced with training their newly hired psychometrist. It supplies concrete guidelines and provides a roadmap for training that can be customized to any practice, department, or clinical setting.

In this essential resource, Dr. Christine S. Ghilain discusses the role of the psychometrist in various neuropsychological practice settings and provides suggested minimum standards of competence across training domains. She dives deeply into the core components of assessment—from optimizing testing conditions, to standardized test administration, to keen observations of behavior—and includes coverage of topics such as testing with unique populations, behavioral management strategies for challenging situations, and promoting ongoing competence over time. A compilation of several sources of data, the book includes excerpts from Dr. Ghilain's practice-specific psychometry training manual along with advice and illustrative examples from many neuropsychologists and psychometrists who shared their experiences.

This book is an indispensable guide for neuropsychologists looking to instill high standards of competence in their hired professionals and for those involved in training graduate students who are just learning to administer cognitive tests. It is also of interest to other assessment-focused professionals looking to enhance their skills and refine their psychological testing knowledge.

Dr. Christine S. Ghilain, PhD, ABPP-CN, is a board-certified clinical neuropsychologist in private practice. Her research and clinical interests include refining assessment practices to enhance diagnostic accuracy and achieve optimal outcomes for individuals with diverse neurological conditions across the developmental life span. She has a passion for training and promoting competence in the field of neuropsychology.

A Neuropsychologist's Guide to Training Psychometrists

Promoting Competence in Psychological Testing

Christine S. Ghilain

Routledge
Taylor & Francis Group
NEW YORK AND LONDON

First published 2022
by Routledge
605 Third Avenue, New York, NY 10158

and by Routledge
2 Park Square, Milton Park, Abingdon, Oxon, OX14 4RN

Routledge is an imprint of the Taylor & Francis Group, an informa business

Library of Congress Cataloging-in-Publication Data
A catalog record for this book has been requested

ISBN: 978-0-367-56498-8 (hbk)
ISBN: 978-0-367-56497-1 (pbk)
ISBN: 978-1-003-09801-0 (ebk)

DOI: 10.4324/9781003098010

Typeset in Bembo
by Apex CoVantage, LLC

To my parents, Ed & Susie Ghilain, for everything.

Contents

Acknowledgments

First and foremost, I am grateful to my husband for his unwavering love, encouragement, and support for this book, as well as every idea this dreamer comes up with.

To my sister, for her impeccable editing skills, among so very many other things—thank you for being such a motivator, mentor, advocate and above all a wonderful best friend.

My sincerest appreciation to Joel Morgan, PhD, ABPP, for introducing me to the Routledge team and for encouraging me to write this book.

Special thanks to the many individuals, both those who chose to remain anonymous and those listed in the contributor section, who shared stories and experiences as psychometrists and neuropsychologists training psychometrists across diverse settings.

Finally, I extend my deepest gratitude to the entire team at Routledge for supporting the publication of this text.

Contributors

The following neuropsychologists and psychometrists provided feedback on their experiences in the field to help inform the book, along with many sources who wished to remain anonymous:

Madison Babula, Psychometrist, Neuro-Psychology Associates of Western Massachusetts, Springfield, Massachusetts.

Mark T. Barisa, PhD, ABPP, Board Certified Clinical Neuropsychologist, Performance Neuropsychology, Frisco/Dallas, Texas.

Magdalene Bracken-Harki, PsyD, Clinical Neuropsychologist, Advocate Lutheran General Hospital, Park Ridge, Illinois.

Christine L. Castillo, PhD, ABPP-CN, NCSP, Pediatric Neuropsychologist, Providence Behavioral Health.

Caroline Conrad, BA, Neuropsychology Technician, Colorado Springs Neurological Associates, Colorado Springs, Colorado.

Danielle Culbreth, MA, Psychometrist, Kaiser Permanente, Atlanta, Georgia.

Jeremy J. Davis, PsyD, ABPP, Associate Professor Clinical Chief, Division of Neuropsychology, Department of Neurology, UT Health San Antonio.

Nance Epstein, MS, CSP, Senior Psychometrist, Seattle Children's Hospital, Department of Rehabilitation Psychology, Seattle, Washington.

Tom Erickson, MA, CSP, NCC, LMHC, Psychometrist, Semi-retired/Private Practice, Seattle, Washington.

Hannah Gallentine, BS, Lead Psychometrist, Nebraska Medicine, Omaha, Nebraska.

Martha Glisky, PhD, ABPP-CN, Neuropsychology and Cognitive Health, Bellevue, Washington.

Kelsey Jackson, MA, Psychometrist, Silver Linings Neurodevelopment, Huntsville, Alabama.

Amber Kippie-Reischman, BA, Psychometrist, Kirk Neurobehavioral Health, Louisville, Colorado.

Denise M. Krouslis, BA, CSP, Neuropsychometrist, Neuropsychology Associates of New Jersey, Morristown, New Jersey

Elizabeth Morgan, PhD, ABPP, Neuropsychologist, Orlando, Florida.

Anastacia Nichols, PsyD, Neuropsychologist, Assistant Professor, Emory University School of Medicine, Division of Rehabilitation Neuropsychology.

Christopher A. Pierce, PhD, Director of Neuropsychology, Denver Health Medical Center, Denver, Colorado.

Leslie D. Rosenstein, PhD, ABPP-CN, Neuropsychologist, UT Southwestern Medical Center and Parkland Outpatient Psychiatry Clinic, Dallas, Texas.

Rachelle Smith, MA, CSP, Psychometrist, WellStar Psychological Services, Marietta, Georgia.

Chelsea Stephens, MA, CSP, Neuropsychology Service, Brooke Army Medical Center, SAMMC, Texas.

Holly Strecker, MA, CSP, Aurora, Ohio.

Anthony Y. Stringer, PhD, ABPP/ABCN, Professor and Director, Division of Rehabilitation Neuropsychology, Emory University, Atlanta, Georgia.

Preface

The process of compiling the resources I would need to write this book sparked a familiar feeling for me. It was a special kind of enthusiasm—the same enthusiasm I felt when studying for what neuropsychologists refer to as "boards," more formally known as the American Board of Professional Psychology's (ABPP) clinical neuropsychology board examination. Back then, it was study outlines, topic lists, stacks of relevant articles, and scores of book chapters; and as I embarked upon the journey of board certification, I endeavored to enjoy the process. I was determined to see studying as an opportunity to hone my knowledge, as opposed to yet another long list of things to check off my checklist. I was legitimately excited to dive into topics with which I had minimal familiarity, as well as share what I was learning with members of my study group.

Perhaps, like me, you went into neuropsychology because the brain bases of behavior fascinated you, and you wanted to help people live their most fulfilled lives. This career path requires many years of training; countless courses on assessment, psychometrics, and psychological theory; and hours of feedback from attending supervisors on how to hone and refine our skills. The process is comprehensive, and at times overwhelming, but it produces practitioners with the skills and expertise necessary to serve patients well.

It was in the midst of that journey, during my internship, that I was first introduced to the role of the psychometrist, and as a student I learned a great deal from the psychometrists with whom I worked. Meticulously trained themselves, these individuals were an asset to my development as a competent test administrator. Later, when my first job required that I hire and train my own psychometrists, I was surprised at the lack of curriculum, benchmarks, or resources available to guide me. As I submit this text to its publisher, there is no standard protocol for training a psychometrist—this despite the fact that a psychometrist's role is a long-standing facet of the field. Speaking informally with colleagues, there seems to be a general expectation that the neuropsychologist will "train" the psychometrist (mostly because the neuropsychologist's license is on the line), but what that training entails, and how that training is enacted, supported, supplemented, and refreshed over time, remains an individualized and largely undiscussed process.

Over the course of my career I have worked in academic medical settings, private hospital systems, and private practices. Each setting provided new experiences: different patient populations, different clinic flow dynamics, and countless opportunities to refine my skills. And in each case, psychometrists were employed, thus providing me with a variety of experiences working with psychometrists and understanding their many job expectations. Each setting also afforded me the opportunity to contribute to the training process, an opportunity that has evolved into a passion over time. As an aspiring lifelong learner, I believe we are all growing from new experiences and opportunities even when our formal training is complete. This text is therefore a compilation of resources for neuropsychologists training psychometrists. My hope is that the information is of use to you or, at minimum, advances conversations around training and competence in psychometry.

Introduction

It is no secret that psychologists wear many hats. Between assessment, therapy, training, research, and consultation, we are fortunate to provide care to our clients via diverse avenues. As neuropsychologists, we use assessment to better understand the brain bases for behavior. While we attended school for many years to hone our skills, I've never heard of psychometrist training included as a component of any required coursework.

This book was initially conceptualized as a guidebook for busy neuropsychologists faced with training their newly hired psychometrist. However, it may also be a resource for graduate student trainees and other assessment-focused professionals looking to enhance their skills and refine their testing knowledge. Nonetheless, given the lack of information about *how* a neuropsychologist should train their psychometrists to date, this book first and foremost endeavors to fill that gap.

Additionally, although I wrote this book from the perspective of a clinical neuropsychologist, I am aware that psychometrists are increasingly being sought out to work in school and other settings. So as not to continually repeat the various professionals who may be training psychometrists (i.e., clinical psychologists, neuropsychologists, counseling psychologists, or school psychologists), please know that each of these titles can be substituted when I discuss the training practices, duties, and responsibilities of the "neuropsychologist." Mentally find and replace "neuropsychologist" with "school psychologist" or otherwise as it best pertains to you.

This book is a compilation of many sources of data, integrated into one condensed training guide. I share my own experiences training and working with psychometrists in various settings, and I also include the thoughts and experiences of many neuropsychologists and psychometrists in the field. In preparing for this book, I sent survey links via professional listservs and group discussion boards to current neuropsychologists and psychometrists (a separate survey for each group). Those who completed it could remain anonymous, as the majority chose to do, or provide contact information for follow-up conversations (those listed in the contributor section). I was humbled by the willingness of colleagues to reflect upon their training processes, as well as psychometrists' willingness to share tips, tricks, suggestions,

DOI: 10.4324/9781003098010-1

those aspects of their training that were successful, and those that could stand to improve.

Let's be honest—if you recently hired a psychometrist, you are likely busy and may be seeking to increase your client load or hoping to maximize your professional time. But how do you train your psychometrist efficiently and comprehensively so they can succeed in their role? This book is designed to answer that question. It provides a training plan, sample handouts, tips, and tricks to make the process of training your psychometrist as painless, comprehensive, and mutually beneficial as possible.

Throughout this text, I reference my practice-specific psychometry training manual that I provide to newly hired trainees. While many pages from that training manual are included in the Appendix, I encourage you to consider creating a manual tailored to your own setting. In the interest of expediting your review of this book and maximizing its utility as a training resource for the busy neuropsychologist, whenever possible, I present information in bulleted form or as a short summary, citing resources for ongoing learning or deeper exploration. Each chapter ends with relevant references, and I'll note that I often ask my psychometrists to read certain articles from those lists. The Appendix contains sample worksheets and handouts to assist with the training process. Given our ever-evolving field, I also encourage readers to head to my website, www.njbrainhealth.com, for updated materials and references.

To be clear, I assume the reader of this text has at least a basic familiarity with psychological assessment. With that in mind, the first two chapters discuss the evolution of psychological testing within the field of neuropsychology, as well as the history of psychometry. Given the long-standing and ever-increasing use of psychometrists by neuropsychologists, a brief history provides context to the reader. Chapters 3, 4, and 5 provide clarity around roles and expectations, a rationale for standardized practices, and cautionary tales against teaching psychological testing via the "passed-down" approach. Chapter 6 discusses psychologists' Code of Ethics and the relevant ethical guidelines that should be reviewed with any psychometrist entering the field.

Chapters 7 and 8 provide the theoretical rationale and practical methods for training psychometrists, respectively. While every training experience should be tailored to the trainee's particular setting, these chapters detail concrete steps to ensure minimum levels of competence.

Chapters 9 and 10 discuss considerations when preparing for the client's arrival and structuring the testing space, while Chapters 11 and 12 focus on the time when the client is in the office for testing. Chapter 11 discusses how to introduce oneself to the client, how to respond to various scenarios that may arise during testing, and behavioral management strategies for challenging situations. Chapter 12 discusses behavioral observations and ways to structure training to maximize keen and diagnostically relevant observations.

Chapter 13 is all about scoring and the creation of score tables. Chapter 14 discusses the impact of diversity on our testing and considerations to take into account when assessing diverse groups, and Chapter 15 reviews potential supplemental responsibilities of psychometrists in various settings. Finally, Chapter 16 is a discussion of best practices to promote ongoing competence in psychometry.

While some may feel disappointed at the lack of chapters on topics such as neuroanatomy or statistics, I encourage neuropsychologists to supplement the training materials contained herein with any they feel are appropriate. It is not to say I don't find those training topics relevant, I simply felt they were not required for an introductory psychometry training guide.

The Benefits of a Psychometrist

A psychometrist can be an invaluable team player that will benefit your practice or department immensely if trained properly; however, untrained or unskilled psychometrists can cause significant, unintended harm to our clients. Perhaps that is a dramatic characterization to some, but if the data we neuropsychologists receive are wrong due to incorrect administration or improper scoring by our psychometrist, we cannot make accurate interpretations, and it is the clients who stand to suffer. Our ethical code of conduct states first and foremost that we will "do no harm," and that is achieved through maintaining the highest standards of training and ongoing supervision of those we entrust to provide care in our practices, departments, or clinics.

None of this is news to you if you've recently hired a psychometrist onto your staff, so let's take a moment to discuss the many ways that a psychometrist can change your practice or department for the better. Putting the training aside for a moment, let's fast forward to a year from now and zoom in on a random day on the calendar. Your psychometrist is highly skilled and excellent in their duties. They administer assessments in a beautifully standardized fashion, keenly note behavioral observations, and deliver a meticulously detailed score table to your desk within 24 hours of the client's testing day.

Let's say, for the ease of this extended example, that you spend ten hours on each case you see. The first hour is an intake session with the client or family; hours two through seven are for testing, scoring, and score table creation; hours eight and nine are your allocated report writing time; and the tenth hour is your feedback session. You have saved six hours of time by hiring a psychometrist, and testing was administered exactly the way you would do it. Zoom out on the calendar and multiply six hours of testing by the four patients you would typically see in a week, and you are now at a 24-hour savings. Perhaps you add a fifth client onto your schedule, and that time savings ramps up to a staggering 30 hours of work time reallocated for different uses. Think of all of the things you could do with 30 more hours each week!

Now, the sample schedule here is not representative of all practices or institutions and does not take into account supervision meetings. Sometimes we have cases that require only a couple hours of testing, and sometimes families require multiple hours of education and support. Thanks to your psychometrist and your newfound schedule flexibility, you more easily can accommodate those connective and supportive conversations when needed. You have the time to read articles and seek tailored recommendations for each of the cases you see, improving the quality of care you provide. Your schedule now offers the opportunity to complete a manuscript or give a talk. Ultimately, you are a better neuropsychologist providing better care to your patients.

Occasions When Neuropsychologists May Want to Complete Testing Themselves

There are many well-respected psychologists and neuropsychologists who do not use psychometrists in their practice and some who raise well-conceptualized arguments against such practice. I wholeheartedly respect both sides of the decision and can appreciate the rationale for not utilizing psychometrists for certain cases, if ever at all. Some feel that without doing the testing for themselves, it is possible that critical behavioral observations may be missed. For example, concerns are valid if a psychometrist misses a slight tremor in a patient who later goes on to develop Parkinson's disease or if language errors are incorrectly attributed to nervousness or age and dismissed instead of recorded. Engaging with the patient during testing is a critical component of the evaluative process.

In another context, those engaging in forensic work share concerns over their ability to testify most accurately without completing the testing themselves. Here again, they reference the ability to make detailed observations during testing that allow them to more confidently argue their case in front of a judge. Often, the qualitative data can be used to demonstrate inconsistencies in how the patient presents versus how their data emerge, and it is the neuropsychologist who ultimately stands to make those arguments in court.

Still others cite preferences against using psychometrists when behavioral concerns or physical limitations make standardized procedures more difficult, if not impossible. Often in these cases, it is the qualitative data that form the report and recommendations, and the quantitative data supplement the observations. In these cases, some neuropsychologists prefer to complete testing on their own or have their psychometrist tag-team the evaluation with both individuals assessing at once.

Further, some argue that allowing poorly or inadequately trained individuals to administer psychological tests has the ability to harm the public and damage the reputation of psychologists more broadly (Turner et al., 2001). Along these lines, they argue that individuals with a bachelor's level credential do not meet level C psychological tests qualifications, as there is an expectation that qualified users have a master's degree in psychology and at least one year of supervised experience. However, the Standards for Educational and Psychological Testing (2014) do acknowledge the possibility that the tests may be administered by individuals with less training and make clear that the scoring, interpretation, and application of results as well as the supervision of administration remain with the qualified user.

With all of that said, I will go out on a limb here and assume that if you are reading, or have read, this book you are interested in or have already hired a psychometrist, and thus I put forth two main points to those who may disagree with the use of psychometrists: (1) a neuropsychologist's work is a direct reflection of the training and support provided to the psychometrist and (2) just because a psychometrist is hired does not mean the psychometrist must be involved in every case. With regard to the first point, high-quality training, engaging discussions on mutually observed behaviors, comprehensive initial training, and subsequent periodic recalibration can do wonders for the data you receive from your psychometrist. With ongoing conversations, particularly around behavioral observations specific to the tests administered, refinement and detail emerge. Naturally, the more patient experience the psychometrist has, the more this skill is refined, but we can do a lot to support the development of this skill over time. The responsibility for high-quality care remains with the neuropsychologist.

With regard to the second point, the psychometrist plays a key role in supporting a more efficient system. Psychometrists are support professionals, extensions of the neuropsychologist, teammates, or collaborators ultimately working under the purview of the neuropsychologists' licenses. There will be times when the neuropsychologist may prefer to conduct the entire evaluation for a multitude of reasons. There is no rule that says if a psychometrist is hired, they are required to be involved in every client visit.

Concluding Remarks

As illustrated here, a well-trained psychometrist can be one of the best investments you make in your practice or one of the most strategic allocations of budgetary funding you can make in your department or clinic. As you'll read in the coming pages, psychometrists have been employed by neuropsychologists since the field's inception, and their use in hospitals, academic medical clinics, and private practices is only increasing as demands for neuropsychological services soar. Given the expected patient loads of some medical settings, it would be extremely difficult to provide high-quality care without a psychometrist.

It is my hope that this book serves as a framework and guide for neuropsychologists training their newly hired psychometrists with the ultimate goal of improving patient care across diverse neuropsychological settings.

References

American Educational Research Association, American Psychological Association, & National Council on Measurement in Education (Eds.). (2014). *Standards for Educational and Psychological Testing*. Washington, DC: American Educational Research Association.

Turner, S.M., DeMers, S.T., Fox, H.R., & Reed, G.M. (2001). APA's guidelines for test user qualifications: An executive summary. *American Psychologist, 56*, 1099–1113.

1 Assessment

The Backbone of the Profession of Neuropsychology

Trends in Psychological Assessment Training

Psychological assessment is a foundational skill and a central component of the identity of clinical psychologists. As such, the American Psychological Association (APA) requires all clinical psychologists to demonstrate competence in psychological assessment at the graduate level (Piotrowski & Zalewski, 1993; Evans & Finn, 2017; Mihura et al., 2017). Some have even argued that psychological testing is the highest technical achievement of psychology (Swenson, 1997). Indeed, graduate programs have been steadily increasing psychological assessment training at the graduate level (e.g., Ready & Veague, 2014). Assessment training also is shifting away from personality measures, toward an increased concentration on neuropsychological measures (Ready & Veague, 2014; Evans & Finn, 2017).

Neuropsychology as a Distinct Subspecialty of Psychology

Neuropsychology has enjoyed incredible growth and solidification as a distinct subspecialty within the broader realm of clinical psychology. Many luminaries worked tirelessly to create models of training, outline minimum competencies, and facilitate the rigorous process of board certification. Newly boarded early career neuropsychologists enjoy the immediate distinction of diplomate status, some without fully appreciating the work that was put in over the past decades to facilitate the attainment of such a distinction.

This first section is a brisk walk through some key moments in the history of psychological testing and the broader field of neuropsychology, up through the Houston Conference. It ends with a lengthier discussion of our current minimum standards of competence that have been outlined over the past couple of years. It is always important to tip our hat to the notable events in the history of our profession as a reminder of where we came from and where we aspire to go next.

To that end, there are many wonderful works extensively detailing the history of neuropsychology from as early as the 1700s (*see* Barr, 2008; Bieliauskas, 2008; Barr & Bieliauskas, 2016; Barr, 2018; Bieliauskas & Mark,

DOI: 10.4324/9781003098010-2

2018; Stucky et al., 2020, among others), and it is fair to say that the history of neuropsychology could easily be a multipart volume in and of itself. Nonetheless, it is amazing to think about what Alexander Luria learned in his lab while studying Russian war soldiers (discussed later) and how these and many other studies conducted would shape testing practices and the field of neuropsychology thereafter. Today, there are daily advancements in neuroimaging, neuroscience, and our understanding of the neuroanatomical correlates of behavior. In tandem, there are advancements in the methods we use to measure these behaviors.

As a starting point, here are a few notable occasions in the early evolution of psychological testing practices and the broader field of neuropsychology:

- 1875: The term "neuropsychology" was first found written or printed in 1875 (*Merriam-Webster*, 2021).
- 1888: Conrad Rieger, a Würzburg neuropsychiatrist, published the first systematic neuropsychological battery (Benton, 2000).
- In the late 1800s, James McKeen Cattell first used the term "mental tests" and was the first to create a standardized test battery that could be used to compare performance across individuals (Cattell, 1890).
- Early in the 1900s, intelligence and psychological testing was used for educational placement, immigration, and military classification but notably lacked the ability to quantify behavioral changes observed in individuals with psychopathology (Barr, 2018).
- Because early psychological testing was so limited, and one test would not capture all brain damage, psychological test batteries in the early 1900s arose out of a desire to characterize the behavioral effects of psychopathology (Barr, 2018).
- Kurt Goldstein studied World War I (1914–1918) soldiers who sustained traumatic brain injuries in battle (Kent, 2020).
- 1919: Shepard Ivory Franz used the first extended psychological battery in a clinical setting at McLean Hospital of Boston (Franz, 1919).
- 1920s: Alexander Luria studied cognition, particularly aphasia, and treated Russian soldiers who sustained traumatic brain injuries in World War II (Greiffenstein & Morgan, 2020). Luria used a case-study approach to treating patients in a highly nuanced, patient-centered, and qualitative neuropsychological assessment method (Kent, 2020). The 1920s were described by E.G. Boring, famous psychological historian, as the "age of mental testing" (Boring, 1950).
- 1921: Hermann Rorschach introduced his inkblot test to diagnose psychological conditions.
- 1930s: Luria's studies of Russian soldiers with brain injuries enabled him to systematically record the modular geography of the brain.
- 1940: The Minnesota Multiphasic Personality Inventory (MMPI) was first published to objectively measure symptoms in psychiatric patients (Hathaway & McKinley, 1943).

- 1940–1950s: Frontal lobotomies and leukotomies were practiced to demonstrate personality changes.
- 1947: Halstead Neuropsychological Battery was created (Halstead, 1947).
- First half of 1900s: David Wechsler and Alfred Binet advocated for the results of intelligence testing to be considered in the context of the examinee's personality, social status, work, and medical histories, which highlighted the importance of both qualitative and quantitative data in assessing intelligence (Kent, 2020).
- 1953: Henry Gustav Molaison, or "H.M.," underwent a bilateral medial temporal lobectomy in an attempt to treat refractory epilepsy. The surgery resulted in dense amnesia due to bilateral hippocampal damage and H.M. became the focus of many neuropsychological studies.
- 1954: Paul Meehl characterized two diverging methods of testing used by psychologists: "statistical" (quantitative) versus "clinical" (qualitative, projective/Rorschach) (Meehl, 1954; Barr, 2018).
- 1963: *Neuropsychologia*, the first journal dedicated to neuropsychology, was published. The second, *Cortex*, was first published in 1964 (Boake, 2008).
- 1965: Normand Geschwind published "Disconnection Syndromes in Animals and Men," a catalog of disconnection syndromes that result from severing the corpus callosum.
- 1967: The International Neuropsychological Society (INS) was formed as the first open-membership organization dedicated to the study of brain–behavior relationships, with its first meeting held in New Orleans in 1973 (Boake, 2008).
- 1974: Luria's patient-centered methods were standardized by Anne-Lise Christensen, resulting in the Luria Neuropsychological Battery.
- 1975: The National Academy of Neuropsychology (NAN) was founded.
- 1976: Muriel Lezak published *Neuropsychological Assessment*, and it was advertised as the first sourcebook on adult neuropsychology (Kent, 2020). He also introduced the concept of a flexible battery approach (Lezak, 1976).
- 1977: INS forms a task force, led by Manfred Meier, on the Education, Accreditation, and Credentialing in Clinical Neuropsychology (Meier, 1981, 1992) focused on the development of educational and training guidelines in professional psychology.
- 1980: Division 40 of the APA (now called the Society for Clinical Neuropsychology) was established; it is now the largest division of APA.
- 1982: ABPP recognized the American Board of Clinical Neuropsychology (ABCN) as a specialty board (Lucas et al., 2014).
- 1988: Edith Kaplan published on the process approach, identifying and discussing multiple processes that could underlie a particular behavior and focusing on the "why" or "how" a failure occurred or score was obtained (Kaplan, 1988).

- 1994: The Association of Postdoctoral Programs in Clinical Neuropsychology (APPCN) was formed.
- By 1995, the Association for Doctoral Education in Clinical Neuropsychology (ADECN) and the Association of Internship Training in Clinical Neuropsychology (AITCN) were formed.
- 1995: The Clinical Neuropsychology Synarchy (CNS) was formed as a consensus voice of the specialty.
- 1996: Clinical neuropsychology was recognized as a psychological specialty, along with clinical, school, and counseling psychology specialties by the Commission for the Recognition of Specialties and Proficiencies in Professional Psychology (CRSPPP; Boake, 2008).
- 1997: The Houston Conference was held on the University of Houston's campus, from which a policy statement was issued outlining recommendations for training beginning at the undergraduate level for those interested in becoming a clinical neuropsychologist (Hannay et al., 1998; Bodin et al., 2016).

The Quest for Competence

Key efforts to detail and measure competence in the field of neuropsychology were undertaken in the late 1990s. In 1998, the Houston Conference Guidelines (HCG) were published, providing the first structured guidance on how to train neuropsychologists, with a focus on the process of specialty training in neuropsychology (Hannay et al., 1998). While this document has served us well for greater than 20 years, efforts are currently underway to update those guidelines given the ways our field has evolved over the past two decades. In addition, the Taxonomy for Education and Training in Clinical Neuropsychology was published in 2017, refining expectations for training at all levels: from graduate coursework through postdoctoral fellowship and ongoing maintenance of certification (MOC; Sperling et al., 2017). It provides a guide to training directors as to the expectations of coursework, didactics, and experiences, and delineates levels of training in neuropsychology from "exposure" to "major area of study."

In the broader field of clinical psychology, the 2002 Competencies Conference: Future Directions in Education and Credentialing is now considered a foundational event for the "competency movement" in professional psychology (Kaslow et al., 2004). A push was made to standardize both foundational and functional competencies across all areas of psychology. Foundational competencies included areas such as knowledge, ethics, individual/cultural diversity, self-reflection/attitudes, and values that are required aspects of all psychologists' training. Functional competencies were defined as specific aspects of professional practice, or what different types of psychologists "actually do" (Rey-Casserly et al., 2012). Within the context of a "cube model" developed by Rodolfa and colleagues, a three-dimensional cube illustrates foundational competencies along the *x*-axis, functional competencies along the *y*-axis, and stages of professional development along the *z*-axis (Rodolfa et al., 2005). In this model, foundational and functional skills are learned and refined over the developmental sequence of training (e.g., graduate, internship, postdoctoral, and continuing education experiences).

Following an initial application of the competence-based cube model of training to the field of neuropsychology in 2012 (Rey-Casserly et al., 2012), the CNS reviewed and updated the model, publishing "Entry Level Competencies in Neuropsychology" (Smith & CNS, 2019). The updated competency model further identifies those training benchmarks that should be achieved at a postdoctoral level.

As neuropsychologists became better known, more clearly defined, respected, and sought out for their unique expertise, many also began to rely on psychometrists to supply one of the most important components of our evaluation: the data. Just as recent efforts in the field have outlined the taxonomy for clinical training and minimum standards of competence in neuropsychology, this book endeavors to begin conversations around minimum standards of competence for psychometrists, to outline a broad taxonomy for training psychometrists, and to share methods to help this process run as smoothly as possible.

References

Barr, W.B. (2008). Historical development of the neuropsychological test battery. *Textbook of Clinical Neuropsychology*, 3–17.

Barr, W.B. (2018). Historical trends in neuropsychological assessment. *Textbook of Clinical Neuropsychology*, 3–13.

Barr, W.B., & Bieliauskas, L.A. (2016). *The Oxford Handbook of History of Clinical Neuropsychology*. Oxford University Press.

Benton, A. (2000). *Exploring the History of Neuropsychology: Select Papers*. New York: Oxford University Press.

Bieliauskas, L.A. (2008). The preparation of the clinical neuropsychologist: Contemporary training models and specialization. *Textbook of Clinical Neuropsychology*, 18–24.

Bieliauskas, L.A., & Mark, E. (2018). Specialty training in clinical neuropsychology. *Textbook of Clinical Neuropsychology*, 14–21.

Boake, C. (2008). Clinical neuropsychology. *Professional Psychology: Research and Practice*, *39*(2), 234–239.

Bodin, D., Butts, A.M., & Grote, C.L. (2016). Postdoctoral training in clinical neuropsychology in America: How did we get here and where do recent applicants suggest we go next? *The Clinical Neuropsychologist*, *30*(8), 1371–1379.

Boring, E.G. (1950). *A History of Experimental Psychology* (2nd Ed.). New York: Appleton-Century-Crofts.

Cattell, J.M. (1890). Mental tests and measurement. *Mind*, *15*, 373–381.

Christensen, A.L. (1974). *Luria's Neuropsychological Investigation*. Copenhagen, DK: Munksgaard.

Evans, F.B., & Finn, S.E. (2017). Training and consultation in psychological assessment with professional psychologists: Suggestions for enhancing the profession and individual practices. *Journal of Personality Assessment, 99*(2), 175–185.

Franz, S.I. (1919). *Handbook of Mental Examination Methods* (2nd Ed.). New York: MacMillan.

Greiffenstein, M.F., & Morgan, J.E. (2020). Important theories in neuropsychology: A historical perspective. *Clinical Neuropsychology Study Guide and Board Review*, 15–30.

Halstead, W.C. (1947). *Brain and Intelligence*. Chicago, IL: University of Chicago Press.

Hannay, J.H., Bieliauskas, L.A., Crosson, B.A., Hammeke, T.A., Hammsher, K.S., & Koffler, S.P. (1998). Proceedings of the Houston conference on specialty education and training in clinical neuropsychology. *Archives of Clinical Neuropsychology, 13*, 157–250.

Hathaway, S.R., & McKinley, J.C. (1943). *Manual for the Minnesota Multiphasic Personality Inventory*. New York: Psychological Corporation.

Kaplan, E. (1988). A process approach to neuropsychological assessment. In M. Dennis, E. Kaplan, M.I. Posner, D.G. Stein & R.F. Thompson (Eds.), *Clinical Neuropsychology and Brain Function: Research, Measurement, and Practice*. Washington, DC: American Psychological Association.

Kaslow, N.J., Borden, K.A., Collins Jr., F.L., Forrest, L., Illfelder-Kaye, J., Nelson, P.D., . . . Wilmuth, M.E. (2004). Competencies conference: Future directions in education and credentialing in professional psychology. *Journal of Clinical Psychology, 60*, 699–712.

Kent, P.L. (2020). Evolution of clinical neuropsychology: Four challenges. *Applied Neuropsychology: Adult*, 1–13.

Lezak, M.D. (1976). *Neuropsychological Assessment* (5th Ed.). New York: Oxford University Press.

Lucas, J.A., Mahone, E.M., Westerveld, M., Bieliauskas, L., & Baron, I.S. (2014). The American board of clinical neuropsychology and American academy of clinical neuropsychology: Updated milestones 2005–2014. *The Clinical Neuropsychologist, 28*(6), 889–906.

Meehl, P.E. (1954). *Clinical vs. Statistical Prediction: A Theoretical Analysis and Review of the Evidence*. Minneapolis, MN: University of Minnesota Press.

Meier, M. (1981). Education for competency assurance in human neuropsychology: Antecedents, models and directions. In S.B. Filskov & T.J. Boll (Eds.), *Handbook of Clinical Neuropsychology* (pp. 754–781). New York: Wiley.

Meier, M. (1992). Modern clinical neuropsychology in historical perspective. *American Psychologist, 47*, 550–558.

Merriam-Webster. (2021). *Neuropsychology*. Retrieved from: www.merriam-webster.com/dictionary/neuropsychology.

Mihura, J.L., Roy, M., & Robert, A. (2017). Graceffo. "Psychological assessment training in clinical psychology doctoral programs." *Journal of Personality Assessment, 99*(2), 153–164.

Piotrowski, C., & Zalewski, C. (1993). Training in psychodiagnostic testing in APA-approved PsyD and PhD clinical psychology programs. *Journal of Personality Assessment, 61*, 394–405.

Ready, R.E., & Veague, H.B. (2014). Training in psychological assessment: Current practices of clinical psychology programs. *Professional Psychology: Research and Practice, 45*, 278–282.

Rey-Casserly, C., Roper, B.L., & Bauer, R.M. (2012). Application of a competency model to clinical neuropsychology. *Professional Psychology: Research and Practice, 43*(5), 422–431.

Rodolfa, E., Bent, R., Eisman, E., Nelson, P., Rehm, L., & Ritchie, P. (2005). A cube model for competency development: Implications for psychology educators and regulators. *Professional Psychology: Research and Practice, 36*, 347–354.

Smith, G., & CNS. (2019). Education and training in clinical neuropsychology: Recent developments and documents from the clinical neuropsychology synarchy. *Archives of Clinical Neuropsychology, 34*(3), 418–431.

Sperling, S.A., Cimino, C.R., Stricker, N.H., Heffelfinger, A.K., Gess, J.L., Osborn, K.E., & Roper, B.L. (2017). Taxonomy for education and training in clinical neuropsychology: Past, present and future. *The Clinical Neuropsychologist, 31*(5), 817–828.

Stucky, K., Kirkwood, M., Donders, J., & Liff, C. (Eds.). (2020). *Clinical Neuropsychology Study Guide and Board Review*. Oxford University Press.

Swenson, L.E. (1997). *Psychology and Law* (2nd Ed.). Pacific Grove, CA: Brooks/Cole.

2 A Historical Overview of the Psychometrist's Role

According to the *Encyclopedia of Clinical Neuropsychology*, a psychometrist is a person trained to administer and score neuropsychological and psychological tests under the supervision of a licensed neuropsychologist or psychologist. Psychometrists also observe the client's behavior during testing (Kurylo & Tsou, 2017).

Psychometry: A Brief History

The evolution of the field of neuropsychology and the use of psychometrists unfolded nearly in tandem. In the late 1930s, William A. Hunt was the first to employ trained "psychological technicians" (an analogous term for psychometrists more frequently used at that time) to administer neuropsychological tests to naval soldiers in World War II (DeLuca, 1989). Ward Halstead and his graduate student Ralph Reitan used technicians in the 1940s at the University of Chicago. Reitan went on to use technicians at the Mayo General Hospital in 1945 and, by the 1950s, established the Neuropsychological Laboratory at the Indiana University Medical School, where he continued to use technicians to support his research and clinical pursuits. Most notably, at that time the duties of the psychological technician were identical to those of psychometrists today—namely, to administer and score psychological tests (DeLuca, 1989).

The use of psychometrists increased exponentially in the 1960s and the 1970s, coinciding with the time when neuropsychology became a distinct subdiscipline of clinical psychology (Malek-Ahmadi et al., 2012). A 1964 article in the *American Psychologist* by Larry Hill details his experiences and reflections as a psychologist who had spent the prior three years training and supervising psychology technicians at the Wilford Hall United States Air Force Hospital (Hill, 1964). Hill acknowledges the possibility that the use of technicians could "under certain conditions . . . lead to superior evaluations" (p. 687; Hill, 1964; Hill & Giffen, 1963). Hill ends his commentary with a statement that training as a psychology technician should begin at the post–high school level, preferably culminating with the attainment of a master's degree, and that the training must be clearly defined and circumscribed

DOI: 10.4324/9781003098010-3

(1964). Nearly six decades later, the training of these individuals remains highly variable and undefined.

Three additional publications about psychological technicians were released in 1974. In the first article, Musante reflected on staff persons' experiences working with technicians. He pointed out how technicians save clinicians' valuable time and how many psychologists believed the testing was completed more efficiently than by faculty and staff. Less patient contact time administering tests led some psychologists to see more patients and allowed others to engage in increased therapeutic or consultation activities (Musante, 1974). Sloop and Quarrick looked at the correlations between psychology technician and psychology graduate student administrations of tests in order to demonstrate the objective reliability of technicians. They detailed the high rates of consistency in terms of administration and scoring of measures between technicians and graduate student trainees on repeated measures administered to the same patients. In some cases, both examiners obtained nearly identical data on the same patient, causing authors to conclude that technicians "can and do perform in an efficient and effective fashion" (p. 218; Sloop & Quarrick, 1974).

In the third article of the series, Gentry wrote about the experiences of a psychology technician from the technician's own perspective. The technician citied appreciation for interactions with senior staff, enjoyment of patient contact and the variety of patients seen, frequent opportunities for learning, and an enhanced sense of responsibility and pride for the work completed as a technician. Frustrations around pressure of the workload, ambiguity of the job description, and a lack of ability to interpret the data they collect were noted by the technician as challenges with the job, although Gentry goes on to acknowledge that often technicians pursued advanced education as a result of their experience. Additionally, Gentry noted that the technicians expressed concerns about a formal training structure and opportunities for professional advancement and salary increases. In my opinion, these articles could have easily been published today with the same issues still highly relevant to the training and use of psychometrists in practice.

In the late 1980s, the focus of professional journal content was on promoting best practices in training, continuing education, and the use of non-doctoral personnel. In 1987, the Division 40 Task Force on Education, Accreditation, and Credentialing (hereafter referred to as "the Task Force") began a series of publications in *The Clinical Neuropsychologist* (TCN) outlining best practices in the field of neuropsychology. First, the Task Force published guidelines on specialized training for neuropsychologists, including graduate, internship, and postdoctoral training expectations. One year later, the Task Force published guidelines regarding opportunities and expectations around continuing education for neuropsychologists. The following year, in 1989, the Task Force issued guidelines regarding the use of non-doctoral personnel in clinical neuropsychological assessment (Division 40 Task Force on Education, Accreditation, and Credentialing, 1989).

The third Task Force publication discusses the common acceptance of the use of psychometrists and highlights the responsibility of the supervising psychologist to "maintain and monitor high standards of quality assurance" (p. 23; Division 40 Task Force on Education, Accreditation, and Credentialing, 1989). It also states that "the selection of tests, interpretation of those tests, clinical interviewing of patients or family members, and communication of test results and their implications *is the sole and exclusive responsibility of the licensed (neuro)psychologist*" (p. 24, emphasis added; Division 40 Task Force on Education, Accreditation, and Credentialing, 1989).

In 1991, the Task Force published the first article describing the educational and training expectations of these "non-doctoral personnel." The article specifies the requirement of a minimum bachelor's degree in psychology, with expectations that a psychometrist complete coursework in areas such as abnormal psychology, personality, statistics, and psychological testing. Those without a degree in psychology are to be given supplemental training and information. Training areas include (1) the administration and scoring of tests; (2) the role of the psychometrist in eliciting best effort of the client and maintaining rapport during testing; (3) ethics; (4) methods for dealing with medical emergencies, attentiveness to statements suggestive of suicidal or homicidal ideation, and general behavior management in the context of testing sessions; (5) thorough understanding of the limitations of the psychometrist's role, being mindful not to present oneself as an independently practicing professional; and (6) discussions around professional relationships (Division 40 Task Force on Education, Accreditation, and Credentialing, 1991). While these training objectives do not deviate significantly from training expectations today, they leave much to be determined in terms of *how* those training experiences are furnished by the psychologist or obtained by the psychometrist.

Despite ambiguity around specific training processes and procedures, the use of psychometrists is quite common today and has been endorsed by clinical psychologists and neuropsychologists for decades. A survey conducted in 1969 by Brodsky and Mixon demonstrated that 16.5% of clinical psychologists used technicians. This percentage rose to 50% by 1986 (Serenty et al., 1986) and 53% by 1993 (DeLuca & Putnam, 1993). The most current salary survey reveals that 53.9% of surveyed doctoral-level neuropsychologists use psychometrists or paid technicians with patients, although many do not use technicians with all patients (Sweet et al., 2020). Nonetheless, surveys of ABCN diplomates show that the overwhelming majority (77.2%) of diplomates supported the professional/technician model (Sweet & Moberg, 1990).

In addition to Division 40 of the APA (Division 40 Task Force on Education, Accreditation, and Credentialing, 1991), several professional organizations have published policy statements endorsing the use of psychometrists, including the American Academy of Clinical Neuropsychology (AACN; Brandt & VanGorp, 1999), the NAN (Axelrod et al., 1999; Puente et al.,

2006), and the Veterans Administration (Puente et al., 2006; Jordan, 1988). In the most recent NAN policy statement, Puente and colleagues outline several recommendations regarding expectations around training and supervision, discussing a minimum educational attainment expectation of a bachelor's degree and the importance of reviewing ethics, Health Insurance Portability and Accountability Act, confidentiality, medical emergencies, neuropsychology and psychopathology, cultural and demographic differences, and the ways that these variables impact test performance and behavior with psychometrist trainees. Further, Puente and colleagues highlight the need for a contractual relationship to be established between technician and neuropsychologist, expectations that the neuropsychologist will maintain adequate liability insurance, and the expectation that the neuropsychologist is available during test administration by a technician. Authors conclude with a statement that, given the standardization of measures, there should be no difference between test administration by a psychometrist and a neuropsychologist (Puente et al., 2006).

National Association of Psychometrists and the Board of Certified Psychometrists

In January 1995, the National Association of Psychometrists (NAP) was formed by a group of motivated psychometrists seeking to build a professional community. The creation of the NAP was an opportunity for psychometrists to engage with each other, discuss issues of professional relevance (e.g., normative updates, administration/scoring questions), and come together as a community. Those seeking additional information to pass along to their psychometry trainees are encouraged to visit their websites at https://napnet.org.

In 2003, a group of psychometrists within NAP created the Psychometry Certification Committee (PCC). This group created educational and experiential requirements that, if met, allowed psychometrists to sit for an examination. Passing of this voluntary examination allowed candidates to identify themselves as Certified Specialists in Psychometry (Kippie et al., 2019). In 2005, the PCC evolved to a standalone entity, the Board of Certified Psychometrists (BCP), although often psychometrists maintain concurrent memberships in both professional groups (Board of Certified Psychometrists, 2021). Once again, those seeking additional information are encouraged to visit their website at www.psychometristcertification.org.

Survey results of current neuropsychologists were mixed in their support of psychometrists attaining certification through the BCP (*see* Hall et al., 2005, for considerations against using psychometrists). Some felt this certification was unnecessary given psychometrists' inability to work independent of a licensed psychologist or questioned the rationale behind studying certain content areas as requirements for success as a psychometrist. Others shared positive experiences of their psychometrists who sat for the exam, while a few shared experiencing ambivalence or a lack of knowledge that this credential existed. Given the mixed support for the BCP certification process, this text maintains the perspective of training by the neuropsychologist, though readers are encouraged to explore both websites for additional information.

Insurance Billing Codes Specifically for Technicians

Yet another sign of support for the use of psychometrists in practice came in 2006. The American Medical Association (AMA) along with the United States' Center for Medicare and Medicaid Services (CMS) published Current Procedural Terminology (CPT) codes that included one code (at the time 96119) strictly devoted to the administration and scoring of assessments by a supervised technician/psychometrist (*see* AMA, 2006a; AMA, 2006b; Puente et al., 2006; Festa et al., 2010). On January 1, 2019, the CPT testing codes were heavily revised, although distinct codes for testing administered by psychometrists were retained (96138 & 96139, *see* APA, 2019). With the delineation of these codes, psychologists or neuropsychologists can bill insurance for the services rendered by a psychometrist.

The Many Terms for Psychometrists

While the scope of psychometrists' duties has not changed significantly over the past 60 years or so, their titles certainly have evolved. Some of the earliest publications referred to these individuals as psychodiagnostic assistants (L'Abate, 1973) or psychological technicians (e.g., Gentry, 1974; Sloop & Quarrick, 1974; Musante, 1974). "Psychometrist" was the preferred term in the late 1980s (Division 40 Task Force on Education, Accreditation, and Credentialing, 1989) and appears to be the one most commonly used today. Still others have referred to these individuals as neuropsychology technicians (DeLuca & Putnam, 1993), testing assistants (Sweet et al., 2015), paraprofessionals (Lowman, 1996), or even psychological extenders (Arkansas Board of Examiners in Psychology, 2000). Across clinical, school, and counseling psychology arenas, a mix of psychological associates, assistants, technicians or aides, as well as school psychological examiners, technicians, assistants, psychometrists, or psychometric assistants, was also used (APA, 1981a, 1981b, 1981c). Throughout this book, I will endeavor to use psychometrist or technician for the sake of consistency.

Analogous Jobs in Other Professions

In the medical field, there are many analogous relationships between doctor and technician. For example, an ultrasound technician performs ultrasounds, obtaining sonogram still images and providing them to the physician for reading and interpretation. Similarly, radiology or electroencephalogram

(EEG) technicians take X-rays or EEGs and provide the scans or data to the physician for use. Technicians in the fields of dentistry and veterinary medicine are highly valuable staff members and are well respected for the work they do. Unlike psychometrists, however, most of these analogous positions have training programs, formal education, and minimum standards of competency. There have been repeated calls for the development of "either formal technician training programs at the BA degree level or increase apprentice-like work opportunities . . . and establishment of some form of national credentialing agency and technician professional organization similar to those currently existing for EEG technicians" (p. 105; DeLuca & Putnam, 1993). This book endeavors to be a step toward more concrete training.

The Benefits of Psychometrists

As previously discussed, many articles discuss the benefits that a well-trained psychometrist brings to a psychological or neuropsychological practice or department, including increased efficiency, enhanced productivity, and increased opportunities to engage in scholarly endeavors (DeLuca & Putnam, 1993). In addition, some argue that a psychometrist minimizes the potential for bias associated with clinical judgment (DeLuca, 1989), as the test administrator can be kept "blind" to diagnosis and can therefore provide "objective" data to the neuropsychologist. It also may allow the psychologist to subsidize the delivery of neuropsychological or psychological services to those patients who otherwise would be unable to access them due to financial or insurance coverage limitations.

There is also the consideration of examiner drift, a well-known result of deviations from standardization due to the lengthy amount of time that can pass between administering psychological tests. Put simply, for those who do not engage in frequent testing, skills understandably become rusty and adherence to standardized procedures becomes muddied. When a psychometrist is hired for a practice or department, their testing skills become second nature and well refined due to the opportunity for daily practice, which ensures the value and validity of the data that are collected.

Working as a psychometrist is a job that many find bring them significant personal and professional pride as well as satisfaction. Many share stories of the diverse patients they work with and acknowledge that, while sometimes the test measures do not vary significantly from one patient to the next, the experience of administering those measures with diverse clients is rarely "cookie cutter." Further, the passion that psychometrists often bring to rapport-building, test administration, behavioral observation, scoring, and training is often invaluable. Through the course of my training and early career, I learned a lot from the highly seasoned psychometrists with whom I worked, and I believe their profession deserves the attention of the professional community of psychologists.

Recent Psychometry Publications

In 2019, Kippie and colleagues published results of a survey detailing the practice settings, job expectations, salaries, and other relevant practice information for psychometrists (Kippie et al., 2019). Authors note that "despite a general approach to training psychometrists, no standardized training or credentialing currently exists" (p. 15; Kippie et al., 2019). Of concern, the most recent research conducted with psychometrists explored their reported quality of life (QOL), noting high levels of emotional exhaustion, burnout, and fatigue in psychometrists across diverse settings (Zane et al., 2020).

Concluding Remarks

Despite its long-standing history spanning nearly eight decades and the acknowledgment of its importance by major professional organizations in neuropsychology, psychometry remains a field characterized by ambiguous definitions, inconsistent titles, and poorly defined training benchmarks (Kippie et al., 2019). I believe that proper training can help alleviate aspects of the burnout and emotional exhaustion that psychometrists experience and that the responsibility to provide training and emotional support lies with the supervising neuropsychologist.

References

American Medical Association (AMA). (2006a). *Current Procedural Terminology Manual.* Chicago, IL: American Medical Association.

American Medical Association (AMA). (2006b). *The Neurobehavioral Status Exam and the Neuropsychological Testing Codes. CPT Assistant.* Chicago, IL: American Medical Association.

American Psychological Association. (1981a). Specialty guidelines for the delivery of services by clinical psychologists. *American Psychologist, 36*, 640–651.

American Psychological Association. (1981b). Specialty guidelines for the delivery of services by counseling psychologists. *American Psychologist, 36*, 652–663.

American Psychological Association. (1981c). Specialty guidelines for the delivery of services by school psychologists. *American Psychologist, 36*, 670–681.

American Psychological Association. (2019). *Psychological and Neuropsychological Testing Codes for Psychologists.* Retrieved March 1, 2021, from www.apaservices.org/practice/reimbursement/health-codes/testing.

Arkansas Board of Examiners in Psychology. (2000). *Use of Psychological Evaluation Extenders/Technicians.* Little Rock, AR: Author.

Axelrod, B., Heilbronner, R., Barth, J., Larabee, G., Faust, D., Pliskin, N., . . . Silver, C. (1999). The use of neuropsychology testing technicians in clinical practice: Official statement of the national academy of neuropsychology. *Archives of Clinical Neuropsychology, 15*(5), 381–382.

Board of Certified Psychometrists. (2021). Retrieved April 13, 2021, from www.psychometristcertification.org/faqs.

Brandt, J., & VanGorp, W. (1999). American academy of clinical neuropsychology policy on the use of non-doctoral-level personnel in conducting clinical neuropsychological evaluations. *Journal of Clinical and Experimental Neuropsychology, 21*(1), 1.

Brodsky, S.L., & Mixon, R.J. (1969). A survey of technician frequency and activities in clinical psychology. *Journal of Clinical Psychology, 25*(2), 221–223.

DeLuca, J.W. (1989). Neuropsychology technicians in clinical practice: Precedents, rationale, and current deployment. *The Clinical Neuropsychologist, 3*(1), 3–21.

DeLuca, J.W., & Putnam, S.H. (1993). The professional/technician model in clinical neuropsychology: Deployment characteristics and practice issues. *Professional Psychology: Research and Practice, 24*(1), 100–106.

Division 40 Task Force on Education, Accreditation, and Credentialing. (1989). Guidelines regarding the use of nondoctoral personnel in clinical neuropsychological assessment. *The Clinical Neuropsychologist, 3*(1), 23–24.

Division 40 Task Force on Education, Accreditation, and Credentialing. (1991). Recommendations for education and training of nondoctoral personnel in clinical neuropsychology. *The Clinical Neuropsychologist, 5*(1), 20–23.

Festa, J.R., Barr, W.B., & Pliskin, N. (2010). The politics of technicians. *The Clinical Neuropsychologist, 24*, 506–517.

Gentry, W.D. (1974). Technicians' views of training and function. *Professional Psychology, 5*(2), 219–221.

Hall, J.D., Howerton, D.L., & Bolin, A.U. (2005). The use of testing technicians: Critical issues for professional psychology. *International Journal of Testing, 5*(4), 357–375.

Hill, L.K. (1964). Some observations on the selection of "psychology technicians." *American Psychologist, 19*(8), 687–689.

Hill, L.K., & Giffen, M.B. (1963). The efficacy of "blind analysis" in psychological evaluations. *Military Medicine, 128*, 185–189.

Jordan Jr., E.J. (1988). Employment of bachelor's-level psychology technicians in the Veterans Administration. In P.J. Woods (Ed.), *Is Psychology for Them? A Guide to Undergraduate Advising* (pp. 149–152). American Psychological Association.

Kippie, A., Ryan, B.J., McManemy, H., Mendina, M.R.E., Porter, P.M., & Malek-Ahmadi, M. (2019). National association of psychometrists: 2015 Professional practices and salary survey of US and Canadian psychometrists. *The Clinical Neuropsychologist, 33*(1), 13–31.

Kurylo, M., & Tsou, J. (2017). Psychometrician. *Encyclopedia of Clinical Neuropsychology*, 1–1.

L'Abate, L. (1973). The laboratory method in clinical child psychology: Three applications. *Journal of Clinical Child Psychology, 2*, 8–10.

Lowman, R.L. (1996). Introduction to the special section on what every psychologist should know about assessment. *Psychological Assessment, 8*, 339–340.

Malek-Ahmadi, M., Erikson, T., Puente, A.E., Pliskin, N., & Rock, R. (2012). The use of psychometrists in clinical neuropsychology: History, current status, and future directions. *Applied Neuropsychology, 19*, 26–31.

Musante, G.J. (1974). Staff evaluations of the technician role. *Professional Psychology, 5*(2), 214–216.

Puente, A.E., Adams, R., Barr, W.B., Bush, S.S., & NAN Policy & Planning Committee. (2006). The use, education, training and supervision of neuropsychological test technicians (psychometrists) in clinical practice. Official statement of the national academy of neuropsychology. *Archives of Clinical Neuropsychology, 21*, 837–839.

Serenty, M.L., Dean, R.S., Gray, J.W., & Hartlage, L.C. (1986). The practice of clinical neuropsychology in the United States. *Archives of Clinical Neuropsychology, 1*, 5–12.

Sloop, E.W., & Quarrick, E. (1974). Technician performance: Reliability and validity. *Professional Psychology, 5*(2), 216–218.

Sweet, J.J., Benson, R.M., Nelson, N.W., & Moberg, P.J. (2015). The American academy of clinical neuropsychology, national academy of neuropsychology, and society for clinical neuropsychology (APA division 40) 2015 TCN professional practice and 'salary survey': Professional practices, beliefs and incomes of US neuropsychologists. *The Clinical Neuropsychologist, 29*(8), 1069–1162.

Sweet, J.J., Klipfel, K.M., Nelson, N.W., & Moberg, P.J. (2020). Professional practices, beliefs and incomes of U.S. neuropsychologists: The AACN, NAN, SCN 202 practice and "salary survey". *The Clinical Neuropsychologist*, 1–74.

Sweet, J.J., & Moberg, P.J. (1990). A survey of practices and beliefs among ABPP and non-ABPP clinical neuropsychologists. *The Clinical Neuropsychologist, 4*(2), 101–120.

Turner, S.M., DeMers, S.T., Fox, H.R., & Reed, G.M. (2001). APA's guide for test user qualifications. *American Psychologist, 56*(12), 1099–1113.

Zane, K.L., McCuddy, W.T., Mahoney, III, J.J., Kelty, M.K., & Scarisbrick, D.M. (2020). Assessing psychometrists' practice to inform neuropsychological services. *Archives of Clinical Neuropsychology*, 1–9.

3 Defining Psychometrist Roles and Expectations

There are different expectations and significant controversy around what is and is not acceptable to ask of a psychometrist. One hears rumors of neuropsychologists "abusing the privilege"—everything from having a psychometrist write entire reports to relying on a psychometrist to select a battery and write behavioral observations for a client, with barely a fleeting glance from the neuropsychologist before signing off on the final report. Survey responses from psychometrists revealed many other role controversies involving testing without on-site supervision and administration of test instruments without any training. In the sections that follow, I will review the wide spectrum of psychometrist duties brought forth in survey responses and offer my own views regarding the appropriateness and ethical considerations involved in determining a psychometrist's role.

Clear Roles and Responsibilities of the Psychometrist

Responses were highly consistent around certain core expectations; both neuropsychologists and psychometrists overwhelmingly agreed that the following are the foundational expectations of psychometrists' duties:

- Test administration
- Scoring
- Score summary table creation
- Notation of behavioral observations
- Test kit management and test supply inventory/ordering

Test administration and scoring are the core job responsibilities of psychometrists, with the creation of a score table being an added expectation for a vast majority of neuropsychologists. Often, the neuropsychologist provides the template for scores and may or may not include relevant information on the score table, including the patient's name, date of birth, date of evaluation, gender/gender identity, race, ethnicity, and age at the time of the evaluation.

DOI: 10.4324/9781003098010-4

Second, noting pertinent behavioral observations, whether on a structured form, via conversation with the neuropsychologist, by typing into a template, or otherwise, is also a clear expectation. While often the neuropsychologist completes some portion of testing or engages with patients at some point during the testing day, psychometrists can provide specific examples or relevant observations during particular tasks to aid in the neuropsychologist's case conceptualization. When working with children, the psychometrist can also be trained in particular behavioral management techniques (see Chapter 12) to guide the neuropsychologist's school-based recommendations. For example, if standing breaks allow the child to focus longer, or the provision of a fidget toy assists with on-task behavior, the psychometrist can note these supports, which then can be translated into functional recommendations for treatment providers.

Finally, there was a consensus around the appropriateness of ordering protocols, inventorying test supplies, and maintaining a general understanding of practice or departmental needs around testing (e.g., knowing when a stimulus book required replacing). Designating one individual to keep tabs on orders, restocking of inventory, and other organizational tasks can reduce confusion and ensure that supplies are readily available when needed.

Roles and Responsibilities Worthy of Ongoing Discussion

The following responsibilities were inconsistently identified and/or are ethically questionable:

- Training of newly onboarded psychometrists
- Training of externs, interns, postdoctoral fellows, and other trainees
- Writing sections of reports
- Involvement in intake interviews or feedback sessions
- Consenting procedures
- Battery creation or on-the-fly alteration of testing processes
- Supervision

Training of newly onboarded psychometrists by senior psychometrists appears to be common practice in many institutions. Particularly if the more seasoned psychometrist was previously trained by the attending neuropsychologist, this can be a way to reduce the training burden on the neuropsychologist and ensure that a thorough review of testing processes and procedures occurs. While this may not be the preferred method of training for some, this can be an effective method if the neuropsychologist subsequently is involved in checking off (i.e., confirming the appropriate testing skills of) the newly trained psychometrist on testing and if the neuropsychologist remains involved with ongoing maintenance of skills (e.g., reviewing files for scoring accuracy/completion every six months, sitting in on portions of client testing to ensure standardization of administration, engaging in conversations surrounding pertinent behavioral observations). While there may be issues making training the sole responsibility of the senior psychometrist, there may be significant time-saving benefits if done appropriately.

Particularly in larger institutions with training programs, psychometrists are often involved in training externs, interns, and other graduate trainees who join the practice or department to gain experience. This can be a wonderful opportunity to engage in a hierarchical training and supervision model, whereby a more seasoned psychometrist reviews standardized procedures with the trainee and the neuropsychologist remains engaged to verify adherence to standardized practices and to subsequently expand upon basic test administration and scoring. Finally, for externs, interns, and graduate trainees, time further is expected to be spent with the neuropsychologist to review interpretation, case conceptualization, report writing, recommendations, and feedback.

Some neuropsychologists ask their psychometrists to write sections of the report, such as filling in a templated behavioral observation section. I would expect the neuropsychologist is also contributing their observations under these circumstances. Still others ask their psychometrists to write background history sections of the report, which I believe is more appropriately the responsibility of the neuropsychologist. Justification for this practice in survey responses included the neuropsychologists' provision of a highly detailed background history form and a templated background history section, but this feels like a slide down a slippery slope from a request to write a couple of report sections to drafting the report in its entirety.

A few psychometrists reported engagement in intake and feedback sessions, though this appeared to be more in a support role than in a leadership role. The rationale was that their involvement allowed them to learn more about the patient, and a few shared that engagement in the feedback session in particular helped them to understand why the neuropsychologist administered the tests that they did, as well as the way the neuropsychologist explained the results of testing to patients. While this may be beneficial for psychometrists aspiring to become neuropsychologists in the future, this raises some concern for the possibility that a psychometrist may then take it upon themselves to interpret or explain data to patients in session. With clear boundaries and expectations set from the beginning, this likelihood is minimized, but neuropsychologists are encouraged to consider both the positives and unintended consequences of including psychometrists on intakes or feedbacks in any capacity.

Particularly in smaller, private practice settings, the psychometrist often doubles as an office manager or front-office staff person. While the consents should always be written by the neuropsychologist (in consultation with a legal entity or malpractice insurance provider), some practices have the psychometrist provide the consent forms and initial paperwork to the client. This can be an appropriate practice as long as the neuropsychologist takes time to review any questions with the client and review his or her understanding of the consent documents prior to engaging in testing.

Survey responses also suggest that some neuropsychologists have their psychometrist create the battery for the client. There are a few isolated cases where this can be considered appropriate. For example, there are some neuropsychologists who take a fixed battery approach, and therefore the psychometrist is doing all the same tests with every patient. Once provided to the psychometrist initially, there is not often a reason to modify the battery, and thus the same battery is used every time. More often, there is a "core" set of assessments that a neuropsychologist uses, and thus the psychometrist is likely to pull those core tests for every client. While some rely upon their psychometrist to consult regarding behavioral observations (e.g., "I noticed X behavior, so do you want me to administer Y measure?"), it is the neuropsychologist who should have the final say in modifying the battery or providing the final test list to the psychometrist.

Some neuropsychologists also report leaving the decision to cut certain measures or end testing sessions early up to their psychometrist. While I am aware that the psychometrist is the one in the room with the patient and spending the bulk of the time attending to the individual, it should fall to the neuropsychologist to make determinations about what to cut, when to call a session, or otherwise. This can and likely should be a collaborative process or a discussion between psychometrist and neuropsychologist, but the ultimate decision should fall to the neuropsychologist.

Finally, there are some psychometrists who report supervising fellow psychometrists or trainees. While the implementation of a hierarchical supervisory model can be extremely beneficial, the neuropsychologist should be actively engaged in the supervision process as well. While a psychometrist can be extremely effective at reviewing standardization of administration or scoring procedures with either trainees or new psychometrists, the neuropsychologist should be the one to review interpretation and conceptualization with trainees. Thus, it falls to the neuropsychologist to structure a supervisory experience that is appropriate for all.

Clearly Inappropriate (and in Some Cases Unethical) Expectations

I find the following requests of a psychometrist to be flat out inappropriate and/or unethical:

- Writing the entire report
- Testing the patient when the supervising neuropsychologist is not on-site
- Providing diagnostic impressions
- Providing feedback to the family or client
- Generating the full test list based on referral questions
- Administering testing without prior training

I'll frame this first one in the context of "training a future neuropsychologist." One survey respondent explained that, when they were working as a psychometrist and preparing to apply to graduate school, they wrote the initial drafts of reports, which then were passed through a series of individuals (more senior psychometrists, postdoctoral fellows, the neuropsychologist). In this structure, the neuropsychologist encouraged the psychometrist to draft the entire report, with diagnostic impressions, data summary, integration of findings, and what I can only assume to be highly templated recommendations. While some justify this decision as appropriate for those psychometrists aspiring to attend graduate school for clinical neuropsychology in the future, I do not believe this is in the best interest of the patient or, quite honestly, the success of the practice or department more broadly. I would discourage the use of this practice, even with the highest levels of supervision and feedback.

Testing while the supervising neuropsychologist is not on-site may be viewed as a gray area for some, but I do not see it as entirely ethical. There were a small number of individuals who shared that they were asked to test patients while their supervisor was not directly on-site. Now, we all have emergencies that arise from time to time, but it is in everyone's best interest to find coverage for on-site supervision or reschedule the patient when these times arise. I cannot think of a situation where it makes sense to have the psychometrist test the patient with no supervisory support on-site. While the neuropsychologist may have conducted the intake and may not have concerns that the client will exhibit violent or aggressive behavior, the process of testing is at times quite stressful, and it is impossible to predict how every client will react to every possible situation. Further, should the client mention abuse, neglect, suicidal ideation/homicidal intentions, or otherwise, the neuropsychologist has a duty to immediately intervene with testing and assess the situation further.

You will notice that there are no sections of this book dedicated to data integration, case conceptualization, or differential diagnosis. These are at the core of the neuropsychologist's job responsibilities and the reason we all went through many years of schooling and fellowship training. It would be impossible to distill all of that down to a quick chapter in a book. Moreover, this is clearly not in the scope of practice for any psychometrist. Thus, despite the fact that some psychometrists identify differential diagnosis as within the scope of their practice, I disagree that this is a component of their job responsibility. I do not wish to discourage psychometrists from thinking about the clients whom they work with or engaging in discussion with their supervising neuropsychologist to understand more about a diagnosis, but the provision of diagnostic considerations by the psychometrist to the neuropsychologist is a poor model of service.

Finally, more than a few psychometrists shared instances where they were asked to administer a test without any formal training or an opportunity to review the test prior to jumping into administration. While some discussed feeling like it was "sort of okay" because they administered similar tests in the past, it is unethical for the psychometrist to be placed in such a difficult situation. Consistent with the expectation that a neuropsychologist is on-site for testing, the neuropsychologist should be able to jump in and demonstrate standardized testing practices for any new or infrequently used measures that a psychometrist expresses concern with administering.

Obvious Roles and Responsibilities of the Neuropsychologist Working With Psychometrists

Much of the feedback I received from psychometrists around their supervising neuropsychologists was appreciation for feeling like a valued member of a team, rather than a cog in a wheel or a robot churning out data. I was struck by the frequency with which survey responders admitted to feeling like "less than a person" because they felt, at times, like they were expected to work long hours and complete work quickly, only to immediately jump into testing another patient the following day. To that end, most of these are common sense, but in the section that follows I will briefly review some of the primary responsibilities we neuropsychologists have in the context of our work with psychometrists. I believe few would argue with expectations around:

- Training the psychometrist in administration, scoring, and data summary sheet production, as well as behavioral observations
- Setting clear boundaries around roles and expectations in the work setting
- Scheduling routine recalibration and spot-checking to ensure competence and mastery of skill, particularly in the early stages of training
- Cultivating an open environment and dedicating a time and space for ongoing supervision, modeling of discussions around accidental administration or scoring errors, review of office or clinic procedures, and professional development
- Modeling appropriate methods for how to work with diverse clients
- Creating the test list and reviewing the client's file
- Writing the report, diagnosing the client, and providing the intake and feedback

Considerations When Working With Psychometrists

Depending on the way that you the neuropsychologist design your practice, you may decide to engage in any or all of the following:

- Administering aspects of testing the client
- Choosing a dedicated observation period of the client above and beyond intake and feedback sessions

- Organizing a hierarchical supervisory model whereby psychometrists participate in the teaching of test administration and scoring to those who rotate through the clinic or practice
- Providing a structured journal club or continuing education opportunities for psychometrists
- Providing funding to participate in conferences or continuing education credits for relevant lectures or topics of interest

Personally, I always complete some of the testing with clients in order to "lay eyes on" the client for myself. I may only do the intelligence testing, which is due to a New Jersey state law forbidding psychometrists from administering intelligence tests, or depending on the reason for testing, I may choose to administer those assessments most relevant to the referral question. I find that I leave my 60-minute or so testing session with plenty of behavioral observations, and it enhances my discussions with the psychometrist at the end of the day.

For those who would prefer, it may be beneficial to observe the client during unstructured time (e.g., in the case of a pediatric client, time with the parent in the waiting room) and/or interview the client toward the end of the testing day (e.g., in the case of a geriatric client, a final wrap-up to determine how they viewed their testing experience). The qualitative data can be just as, if not more, rich than the qualitative data, and thus time spent with the client above and beyond the psychometrist's formal testing is important.

There are some large, academic medical centers or group practices that employ a team of psychometrists. This is a wonderful model, as it allows the psychometrist opportunities to consult with colleagues and to enhance their training through engagement with similar professionals. Often in these settings, psychometrists are also tasked with training externs, interns, or other trainees on the proper administration and scoring of various neuropsychological tests. A hierarchical supervision model, whereby trainees are supervised by psychometrists, who are then supervised by a neuropsychologist, can provide opportunities for enhanced skill development across levels of professionals.

Journal clubs or dedicated meetings to stay up on the bourgeoning assessment literature can be a wonderful way for everyone to keep up with advancements in the field. While no one wants to add yet another meeting to their schedules, this doesn't have to be another chore. When possible, having a coffee or breakfast meeting, or convening in a local park (as long as there are no patient-specific conversations), to discuss a new article can make the task less cumbersome and more enjoyable for all.

Finally, supporting a psychometrist's interest in honing their skills or advancing their knowledge will benefit you and your patients alike. I have worked with a few stellar psychometrists who went above and beyond to streamline practice processes and procedures, or who have brought new editions of tests or questionnaires to my attention before the email alert from the testing companies was sent. Making room in the budget for your psychometrist's professional development is a worthwhile consideration if practice or department funding allows.

Inappropriate Requests and Clear Abuse of Power in the Psychometrist/Neuropsychologist Relationship

This end of the spectrum is generated from responses of psychometrists about things they did not feel comfortable conveying to their neuropsychologist. As a good working relationship makes for a better work environment and better results, it is important to be mindful of and avoid the following:

- Responding to inquiries about the test list with "Because I said so" as a response to why certain tests are given, making the psychometrist feel belittled and embarrassed for asking
- Setting rigid deadlines with no flexibility or consideration for the psychometrist's experience
- Making the psychometrist feeling like a robot, cog in a wheel, or "less than" a person because they do not have the same credentials as a neuropsychologist
- Asking the psychometrist to engage in tasks outside of their bounds of competence, particularly given the power differential
- Neglecting basic needs such as restroom breaks or a dedicated break time for lunch

Multiple respondents expressed concern that psychometrists can be made to feel like work horses. Their job is very important and does involve long spans of time engaging with clients, but we want to support their experience when they are feeling distressed. Situations seem to frequently arise where a psychometrist notes a client becoming increasingly frustrated or upset with their performance on tests. The psychometrist typically then goes to the neuropsychologist to discuss any reduction of the battery, and the neuropsychologist often responds with "no, I need it all, just get it finished." This can feel disheartening to a psychometrist, particularly as they face the brunt of the increasingly dysregulated client across from them. In these moments, it may be helpful to suggest a break, discuss options for returning to finish testing, or genuinely consider battery modification when clinically appropriate. It is possible that a change to the remaining testing tasks is impossible, but providing support to the psychometrist and offering suggestions around how to continue testing (while gathering good data) are paramount in these times.

As alluded to earlier, psychometrists noted times when they felt their neuropsychologist expected them to be a robot, to plod forward with testing despite increasing agitation from clients, or to have score tables generated in a seemingly unreasonable amount of time following the conclusion of the client's appointment. While we all have those days where we just need to keep our heads down and charge forward through an insurmountable number of tasks, this point highlights the need for us to set specific expectations regarding score table generation following the completion of the testing. We also want to cultivate an environment where the psychometrist feels comfortable sharing if the timeline can't be met for whatever reason. Red flags may go up if there are repeated requests for extensions, but recognizing that certain clients can elicit emotional experiences or stressful responses in our psychometrists is important. It may be that the psychometrist needs to step away from the client's file for 24 hours and return to it when they feel ready to do so. Cultivating an environment where stressful or difficult experiences can be discussed or at minimum acknowledged can go a long way toward strengthening the team as a whole.

At times, we may inadvertently ask our psychometrists to engage in tasks outside of their comfort zones. Take, for example, a request to administer a test the psychometrist has never seen before. "Here, it is really straightforward, I am sure you can quick review it during lunch and add it to the battery. It's just like X test, and you've given that hundreds of times." This is certainly a scenario that can arise, and perhaps is one that is less egregious than others I have heard, but in this moment the psychometrist may not feel comfortable stating that they do not feel ready to administer a test they've never reviewed. I would encourage the following tweak to the scenario, which may or may not end with the same result. "Here is a test I'd like to add to the battery this afternoon. Do you think you'd have time to review it, or would you like me to administer it and you can observe?" Particularly if it is similar to a test they've already administered, this request may be appropriate. However, often psychometrists use their lunch hour to get a jump on scoring or dare I say eat and take a mental health break, so adding this request may feel overwhelming. Again, cultivating open communication whereby the individual can freely state if they feel uncomfortable promotes a healthy climate in the workplace.

Finally, I was intrigued by how often psychometrists report being made to work through their lunch hour, quickly downing a granola bar or some sort of snack during a break, and eating their lunch when the client left at 3:00 or 4:00 p.m. If this is the psychometrist's preference, great, but acknowledging the importance of meeting basic human needs is worthy of thought before dictating the schedule of psychometrists in your office or clinic. Sometimes modeling our own self-care (take a mental survey of how often you've eaten at your own desk!) can be a great way to cultivate a healthy work climate in our offices.

Concluding Thoughts

This chapter is not intended to be an exhaustive list of all possible duties and responsibilities of either the psychometrist or the neuropsychologist and my personal views for or against them. The goal is to review common expectations and frequent requests, while simultaneously encouraging thoughtful consideration of the requests we make of our psychometrists. It further encourages the upholding of the highest standards of professionalism for both neuropsychologists and psychometrists alike. Often, it boils down to professionalism, respect and open communication, and the cultivation of a culture that holds these ideals in high esteem.

4 Pitfalls of the "Passed-Down" Approach to Training in Psychological Testing

Graduate training in assessment can be somewhat narrowly focused. Particularly given the lack of formalized educational requirements of psychometrists, it is our responsibility to engage fully in the education and training of the individuals we hire. Too often I have heard stories of assessments being incorrectly administered for years, simply because the original administrator was taught incorrectly and no recalibration efforts were undertaken. In this chapter, I will review a few clear examples of why the "passed-down approach" of simply learning from someone else without consultation with the test's published manual perpetuates poor assessment practices. I will touch upon "examiner drift" and the likelihood that if you have been away from testing, there are many specifics that you may forget or misremember. The ultimate goal of this chapter is to provide a rationale for returning to the manuals and to setting up systematic review practices to ensure ongoing standardization and competence.

Return to the Source

It can be hard enough walking into a new job with one boss, but if you have hired a psychometrist and there are many neuropsychologists in either your practice or your department, expectations around job performance can quickly go from clear to muddy. I can recall during my training a few isolated instances when one supervisor taught me a particular way to administer a test, another taught me a slightly different way, and the manual described a completely different method of administration altogether. These inconsistencies make it hard for psychometrists and trainees to meet training expectations and can cause frustration, anxiety, and defensiveness. Most concerningly, variability raises immediate questions regarding the validity of any data obtained. Thus, my recommendation is to orient your psychometrist to the original sources of critical data from the outset of training. It is our responsibility to guide psychometrists to the administration manuals that accompany most assessments, and review with them the places where they can find answers to administration questions and verify

DOI: 10.4324/9781003098010-5

correct testing methods at any time. As a bonus, psychometrists will then be in the habit of seeking the source prior to darkening your doorstep with questions about administration, and they will know where to go and how to find the answers. In the case of newer assessments, publishers furnish manuals with their assessments, and the manual is a one-stop reference for general test information, standardized administration, and scoring. Within the pages of those texts, specific methods of administration are clearly outlined. This reduces confusion and frustration, and assists the psychometrist in learning that standardization is best followed when taken from the publisher's materials, rather than how a supervisor recalls giving it "back in the day." For tests that do not have a readily available manual, I strongly encourage review of information contained in the most recent version of Strauss and colleagues' *A Compendium of Neuropsychological Tests* (3rd edition, Strauss et al., 2006; 4th edition, Sherman et al., 2021).

Stories of "How I Was Taught"

There was no shortage of stories from survey responders and colleagues detailing disagreements on the methods of administration of one test or another. In one instance, a psychometrist shared that she was reprimanded for providing feedback regarding accuracy of responses (correct/incorrect) to a patient on the Test of Memory Malingering (TOMM). After carefully reviewing the manual, she met with the neuropsychologist who realized many accidental years of incorrect administration.

In another instance, a psychometrist was taught to immediately provide the stimulus cue on the Boston Naming Test (BNT), at the same time as the presentation of the picture. In this way, the client never truly spontaneously named any item, and this continued until a graduate student questioned the method.

Other notable examples from anonymous survey respondents include:

- Allowing a patient to prop up the back half of the book when viewing Judgment of Line Orientation (JOLO) stimuli
- Neglecting to add demographic point adjustments to JOLO scores
- Incorrectly administering grip strength
- Administering grooved pegboard with the pegboard upside down
- Never querying when administering the Wechsler verbal subtests
- Not observing timing considerations in cuing on the BNT
- Never administering the multiple-choice section of the BNT, or the recognition portion of testing on the Wechsler Memory Scales, Fourth Edition (WMS-IV), or Rey Complex Figure Test (RCFT)
- Incorrectly presenting the iPad causing Wechsler block design and WMS-IV Visual Reproduction stimuli to be viewed upside down

Encouragingly, most neuropsychologists who were willing to acknowledge that they were incorrect in teaching a test via the "passed-down approach" were also quite willing to admit that they were wrong and that they were appreciative of the psychometrist who brought the error to their attention. We are all human, we all make mistakes, and we all deserve some grace when we recognize our errors and attempts to fix them. Therefore, empower your psychometrist to critically review testing manuals and to speak up if errors in administration or scoring are observed.

As a trainee, I once had a supervisor who was more than happy to correct an error or to review a manual with me if he noticed I had administered something incorrectly. He was kind in not reprimanding me in front of the client, and was pleasant in our conversations about how I should have administered the test. However, it was also very well known that the kindness was only extended the first time. If you did not internalize the mistake and correct it thereafter, a less pleasant conversation was coming your way the second time the error was observed—a powerful motivator to learn quickly. I use this model when training psychometry staff in my own practice. If a mistake happens, I go out of my way to support the psychometrist in understanding their error and the ways to correct it going forward. I take the time to review a manual or pull pertinent articles to support their understanding, as needed. I then expect the mistake not to occur again and am pleased to say that in my experience, I have rarely required that "second conversation."

It is also important to critically evaluate the skills of a psychometrist trained by a different neuropsychologist. For example, a few survey respondents discussed observing recently hired trainees from other institutions administering tests incorrectly despite many years of practice. Other survey respondents pointed out that the ambiguity of certain test directions can result in variations in administration procedures over the years. Thus, it is encouraged that all psychometrists, regardless of prior training or background, engage in some level of a check-off process to verify accuracy in test administration as they start in a new practice or department. In cases where variations arise, it is best to determine a group consensus among neuropsychologists and psychometrists within your practice or department so as to keep procedures consistent within a department or clinic.

Combatting Examiner or Administration Drift

Examiner or administration drift is the accidental movement away from standardized practices over time due to infrequent administration or misremembering of specific prompts or test directions. It is not intentional, but it occurs when a test administrator relies upon their own memory when providing directions, instead of returning to the manual and reading test prompts verbatim. Often, test administrators feel confident that they recall the exact wording from the manual, but over time, they begin to inadvertently change occasional words or paraphrase directions.

How can we ensure that not only the proper administration guidelines are followed from the outset of training but also that they are maintained and recalibrated through the psychometrist's tenure with your office or department? Active engagement. I know of some departments where yearly recalibration meetings are held to refresh all neuropsychologists and psychometrists about proper administration of the most commonly used tests. In Chapter 7, I will outline a method of initial training and provide insight into options for ongoing maintenance of skills. While I'd argue this is important for both neuropsychologists and psychometrists alike, there are some who may prefer to have psychometrists engage in recalibration efforts alone.

When a question arises around standardized administration, neuropsychologists have the opportunity to model how we would like it addressed. Returning to the manual with the colleague or psychometrist, reviewing where administration directions are typically included, verifying the process, and subsequently following up with others in the department or office can set the stage for methods to address these inconsistencies going forward. Particularly in larger practices or departments, a quick email can be a great way to remind the team of the best practices and procedures when specific questions arise.

Another option is to hold a routine teaching seminar, whereby a neuropsychologist, psychometrist, or even trainee reviews a frequently used test, its administration and scoring. This dedicated time can also be used to present particularly challenging cases of scoring (e.g., a very complicated RCFT drawing) or to discuss a new test that is recently purchased for the team's use. While I know none of us want to add one more meeting to our calendar, quality assurance procedures are a worthwhile way to spend our time.

I have also learned of some departments that block one day per year to recalibrate on all the major measures used within their clinic. I applaud this dedication to best practices.

At times, questions arise about tests that are not commonly included in a standard battery. Listservs from major national and international groups (e.g., American Academy of Clinical Neuropsychology) make verification of standard practice a quick and relatively painless process. For those psychometrists involved in the National Academy of Psychometry, listserv membership is also an opportunity to reach out to a community of psychometrists who are willing to share their experience.

Final Thoughts

Our data are only as good as the methods by which we procure them, and if we are not following standardization, we risk incorrect data, misinterpretation, and unintended harm to the patients we serve. That said, there are some tests where multiple administration methods are valid, and thus conversations and consensus around the methods of administration should be agreed upon. When in doubt, refer back to the manual.

References

Sherman, E., Tan, J.E., & Hrabok, M. (2021). *A Compendium of Neuropsychological Tests: Fundamentals of Neuropsychological Assessment and Test Reviews for Clinical Practice* (4th Ed.). New York: Oxford University Press.

Strauss, E., Sherman, E., & Spreen, O. (2006). *A Compendium of Neuropsychological Tests* (3rd Ed.). New York: Oxford University Press.

5 Standards and Standardization of Testing Procedures

The most recent edition of the Standards for Educational and Psychological Testing (hereinafter referred to as the Standards) was released in 2014. The Standards are the product of the Joint Committee, a team of 15 professionals representing three primary sponsoring organizations, including the APA, the American Educational Research Association (AERA), and the National Council on Measurement in Education (NCME). At least one board-certified (ABPP) neuropsychologist participated as a joint committee member, and organizations including the American Academy of Clinical Neuropsychology (AACN) and National Association of Neuropsychology (NAN) were provided with opportunities to make comments on early drafts.

The Standards were created to "promote sound testing practice and to provide a basis for evaluating the quality of those practices" (p. 1; AERA et al., 2014). While the text includes standards relevant to test creation, reliability, validity, and interpretation, it also provides standards for test administration, aspects of scoring, as well as rights and responsibilities of both test users and test takers. The Standards are a comprehensive guide for sound testing practices and thus a relevant reference for practicing psychometrists. Even though many standards are not relevant to the work of practicing psychometrists, I recommend making a copy of the Standards available to all psychometrists as a reference. Here, I will review the Standards that are *most* relevant to psychometrists.

Before walking through specific chapter content, it is worthwhile to consider the definitions of key terms. As reviewed in the Standards:

- **Test**: "a device or procedure in which a sample of an examinee's behavior in a specified domain is obtained and subsequently evaluated and scored using a standardized process" (p. 2; AERA et al., 2014).
- **Assessment**: "a broader term than test, commonly referring to a process that integrates test information with information from other sources (e.g., information from other tests, inventories, and interviews; or the individual's social, educational, employment, health or psychological history)" (p. 2; AERA et al., 2014).

DOI: 10.4324/9781003098010-6

Thus, psychometrists administer tests as part of a neuropsychologist's assessment.

An Overview of the Standards Most Relevant to Psychometrists

Standards Chapter 3: Fairness in Testing

Broadly, the standards in Chapter 3 refer to maximizing fairness and minimizing construct-irrelevant barriers to maximal performance. While it is the neuropsychologist's responsibility to generate an appropriate test battery based on the client's characteristics (i.e., race, ethnicity, gender, language, age, culture, disability status, socioeconomic status), it is critical for test users/administrators to be aware of and attuned to individual differences that may compromise validity in testing. As the Standards clearly outline, following standardized administration procedures, uniformly reciting specified directions, maintaining specified time limits, and employing other standardized procedures reduce the likelihood that administration conditions influence the performance of some test takers and not others. While there are some instances where a test administrator may be justified in deviating from standardized procedures, thereby gaining a more accurate measurement of the client's ability on a particular construct, deviations from standardized practice must be documented and communicated to the neuropsychologist so that accurate interpretation can occur.

In general, it is best to teach standardized methods of administration and encourage psychometrists to consult with their attending neuropsychologist in cases where alterations to standardized procedures are felt to be warranted. Standard 3.0 is an overarching standard valuing the minimization of construct-irrelevant variance and promoting valid score acquisition for all test takers. Standard 3.4 acknowledges the importance of comparable treatment of all test takers on the same measure, thus reinforcing the need to stick with standardized procedures as outlined by test manuals. Standard 3.9 touches upon appropriate accommodations for measuring the client's true abilities and a construct, and Standard 3.10 discusses the importance of documenting any accommodations or modifications made to standardized administration. Finally, Standard 3.14 reviews considerations when working with interpreters.

Standards Chapter 6: Test Administration, Scoring, Reporting, and Interpretation

The standards outlined in Chapter 6 discuss test administration, scoring, reporting, and interpretation. Standard 6.0 speaks directly to the responsibility of neuropsychologists to adequately train and support psychometrists using testing measures. It also discusses the importance of documenting and, where possible, correcting test administration errors that occur.

Standards Chapter 9: The Rights and Responsibilities of Test Users

Arguably one of the most important chapters to be reviewed by a psychometrist, Standards Chapter 9 reviews the rights and responsibilities of test users. Standard 9.0 hones in on the importance of maintaining test security, while 9.2 emphasizes the need to be familiar with and understand the use of materials that come with each test instrument. Standard 9.5 acknowledges the possibility of scoring errors and the need to monitor accuracy during scoring. As was discussed in Standards Chapter 3, Standard 9.9 reminds us of the importance of documenting any alterations of format so it can be validated. Similarly, Standard 9.14 states that if a reasonable accommodation is available to a client, the individual should be made aware of that option. Finally, Standards 9.19, 9.21, and 9.22 discuss the protection of client privacy, security of tests, and copyright of tests.

Standards Chapter 10: Psychological Testing and Assessment

Standards Chapter 10 emphasizes test administration. Standards 10.1 and 10.3 remind test users of the importance of practicing within one's bounds of competence and emphasize the importance of training in the requisite knowledge and skills required to administer tests. Similar to those standards discussed in Standards Chapter 9, Standards 10.8 and 10.18 discuss the need to follow instructions as they are written, and to maintain the confidentiality of test materials and test results.

I want to again emphasize that the entire Standards book is a resource to psychometrists and anyone administering and scoring tests. It is possible that other standards may apply to your practice, or may be particularly relevant to the patient population you work with. Nonetheless, given the importance of standardized administration, the standards reviewed here are a great starting point for early psychometry trainees.

When Standardization Is Not Followed

In some cases, modifications to standardized approaches are appropriate (see Chapter 14 for a discussion of accommodations and modifications to testing for certain populations, and the importance of documenting changes to standardized procedures). Often a manual will discuss methods of deviation from standardize procedures or provide appropriate accommodations or modifications that do not substantially impact the interpretation of obtained scores. For example, often there is some level of appropriate clarification of task demands during a training or practice question.

However, when unstandardized methods are unintentionally used, the validity of the results may be compromised, particularly when results obtained via unstandardized methods are scored using normative data that assumes standardized administration. In this chapter, I review a few examples of ways that unstandardized assessment methods, even the slightest of deviations, can drastically alter the data obtained.

In 2003, an article was published in the *Journal of Forensic Neuropsychology* entitled, "Standardized Test Administration: Why Bother?" (Lee et al., 2003). This article is a staple on my psychometrist training reading list. The article provides numerous examples of how even the slightest deviation from standardization can change the scores obtained in the context of forensic neuropsychological assessments. For example, reading digits on a digit-span task more rapidly than one per second results in inflated scores (Baddeley & Lewis, 1984; Lee et al., 2003), as does dropping one's inflection on the final digit of a digit-span task (Hagen et al., 1977; Lee et al., 2003). Inflated scores could then be misinterpreted by the neuropsychologist, leading to the potential for misdiagnosis or a mischaracterization of the client's true abilities.

These issues are not limited to the forensic realm; recent research confirms that there are ongoing issues surrounding errors on academic achievement measures (Harrison et al., 2019) and intelligence measures (Styck & Walsh, 2016; McDermott, Watkins & Rhoad, 2014) in clinical settings as well. Thus, ongoing training and recalibration efforts are wholly worthwhile and necessary to promote excellence in administration and scoring.

Third-Party Observers as Threats to Standardization

There is no shortage of literature discussing the impact of third-party observers on neuropsychological testing. For those interested, I include policy statements and relevant literature to peruse in the references (e.g., National Academy of Neuropsychology, 1999a; National Academy of Neuropsychology, 1999b). Nonetheless, as discussed in the American Academy of Neuropsychology's 2001 policy paper, the possibility exists for multiple adverse effects when a family member, lawyer, or other individual is permitted to remain in the room during testing of a client (American Academy of Clinical Neuropsychology, 2001). This threat can be due to social facilitation (McCaffrey et al., 2005) or other external factors and can invalidate testing results.

The only notable exception to this rule pertains to parents who may remain in the testing room for toddlers and other young children. Often, there is difficulty separating young children from caregivers, to the point where it may invalidate the results if the parents are not in the room providing support to the neuropsychologist or psychometrist, at least in the initial stages of testing. Often once a rapport has been established, parents are able to slip out of the room unnoticed (American Academy of Clinical Neuropsychology, 2001).

Standardization Versus Testing Limits

Although discussed at length in Chapter 12, there is a notable difference between breaking standardization and testing the limits (i.e., waving time limits or altering standardized procedures to see if a client can perform better under different conditions). There will be times when a client is over the expected time limit or is close to the completion of a task when it may be appropriate to allow the client the momentary success of completing the task. This may be important for rapport-building or may provide key behavioral data. While the score will not reflect the client's correct answer, it can be helpful to note how frequently a client is correct after a time limit lapses in order for the neuropsychologist to distinguish inability to complete a task due to cognitive limitation, from inability to complete the task due to reduced speed of processing. In the early phases of training, I hold off on the discussions of limit testing, as I would like the psychometrist to focus on standardization first. That said, by the time they are testing independently, we have discussed the appropriate use of limit testing, and the psychometrist has likely observed me testing the limits with several clients.

References

American Academy of Clinical Neuropsychology. (2001). Policy statement on the presence of third-party observers in neuropsychological assessment. *The Clinical Neuropsychologist, 15*(4), 433–439.

American Educational Research Association, American Psychological Association, & National Council on Measurement in Education (Eds.). (2014). *Standards for Educational and Psychological Testing*. Washington, DC: American Educational Research Association.

Baddeley, A., & Lewis, V. (1984). When does rapid presentation enhance digit span? *Bulletin of the Psychonomic Society, 22*, 403–405.

Hagen, R.L., Durham, T., & Shannon, D. (1977). Administration of digit span in the Wechsler and Binet: Differences that matter. *Journal of Clinical Psychology, 33*, 480–482.

Harrison, G.L., Goegan, L.D., & Macoun, S.J. (2019). Common examiner scoring errors on academic achievement measures. *Canadian Journal of School Psychology, 34*(2), 98–112.

Lee, D., Reynolds, C.R., & Willson, V.L. (2003). Standardized test administration: Why bother? *Journal of Forensic Neuropsychology, 3*(3), 55–81.

McCaffrey, R.J., Lynch, J.K., & Yantz, C.L. (2005). Third party observers: Why all the fuss?. *Journal of Forensic Neuropsychology, 4*(2), 1–15.

McDermott, P.A., Watkins, M.W., & Rhoad, A.M. (2014). Whose IQ is it? —Assessor bias variance in high-stakes psychological assessment. *Psychological Assessment, 26*(1), 207.

National Academy of Neuropsychology. (1999a). Presence of third-party observers during neuropsychological testing. *Archives of Clinical Neuropsychology, 15*(5), 379–380.

National Academy of Neuropsychology. (1999b). Test security: Official position statement of the national academy of neuropsychology. *Archives of Clinical Neuropsychology, 15*(5), 383–386.

Styck, K.M., & Walsh, S.M. (2016). Evaluating the prevalence and impact of examiner errors on the Wechsler scales of intelligence: A meta-analysis. *Psychological Assessment, 28*(1), 3–17.

6 Ethics

Promoting Excellence Within the Bounds of Competence

As licensed psychologists, we are bound by the APA's Ethical Principles and Code of Conduct (hereinafter referred to as the Ethics Code; American Psychological Association, 2017), as well as various state-level statutes and regulations. With required continuing education credits for ethics mandated across many states, these guidelines, rules, and regulations are some of the most important documents of our professional practice. Given that a psychometrists' work is directly subsumed under our state licenses, it is of the utmost importance that psychometrists review both the APA Ethics Code and the various state standards that are applicable to psychologists. As an extension of my work, I expect my psychometrist to be held to the same standard of ethical practice as I uphold each day.

Here is a summary of the ethics review I include in my practice's psychometry training manual. While again, not all neuropsychologists prefer to create a manual, this highlights the specific principles and codes of conduct most relevant to psychometrists and their work with clients. Although there are many aspects of the ethics code that do not directly pertain to psychometrists, the following aspects of the ethics code are particularly relevant to psychometrists. I also provide supplemental chapter readings or articles that allow us to expand upon relevant conversations (e.g., Brickman et al., 2006).

APA Ethical Principles and Code of Conduct

Although psychometrists are not licensed psychologists or neuropsychologists, their work is directly subsumed under the license of these professionals. Psychometrists work as an extension of the licensed professional. Therefore, psychometrists should be expected to abide by and to uphold the APA's Code of Conduct in their professional capacity. Comprised of General Principles and Ethical Standards, the general principles outline aspirational goals for the highest ideals of psychology, and the ethical standards delineate enforceable rules of conduct. While this is not meant to be an exhaustive summary detailing all components of each principle or standard, the most relevant and applicable components to psychometry and its practice are reviewed. Psychometrists are strongly encouraged to review the

DOI: 10.4324/9781003098010-7

full APA Ethics Code as well as the full series of state statues in the state in which they practice.

General Principles of the APA Ethics Code

Principle A: Beneficence and Nonmaleficence—In essence, this principle states that we shall "do no harm" to those individuals with whom we work. Should conflicts arise, we take steps to resolve the conflict in a reasonable way and in a way that either avoids or minimizes harm. Importantly, it also states that we maintain awareness of the state of our own physical and mental health and to be aware of the ways that our own health impacts our ability to help others.

Principle B: Fidelity and Responsibility—We establish trusting relationships with those with whom we work, and uphold the highest possible professional standards of conduct. We take responsibility for our actions and take care to resolve conflicts of interest that could lead to harm. We work with others to best serve those with whom we work, and we expect our colleagues to uphold similar standards of professional conduct. We strive to offer some of our services for little to no compensation.

Principle C: Integrity—We promote accuracy, honesty and truth in our activities. We keep promises made and avoid questionable or unclear commitments. If deception is required, we maximize benefits and minimize harm. Any mistrust or unforeseen harmful effects are the direct responsibility of the psychologist to correct.

Principle D: Justice—All people are entitled to access and benefit from our services. All people deserve to be treated equally and comprehensively. We take care to understand our own biases, the boundaries of our own competence, and our own limitations to ensure fair and just practices for all.

Principle E: Respect for People's Rights and Dignity—We respect the rights, welfare, dignity, and worth of all people, and we are particularly aware of the need to protect individuals in vulnerable populations. We acknowledge and respect all differences, whether based on race, ethnicity, age, gender, gender identity, culture, religion, sexual orientation, language, disability status, socioeconomic status national origin, or otherwise, and take these differences into account when working with individuals. We acknowledge our own biases and how our biases can impact the work we do.

Ethical Standards

Ethical Standard 1: Resolving Ethical Issues—The sub-standards of Ethical Standard 1 are all focused on representing one's true self, acting in an ethical and responsible manner, taking steps to correct incorrect information put out into the world, and holding others to high standards of practice. Many of the sub-standards pertain to responding to and complying with any ethics violation brought against the psychologist. In the same vein, psychometrists should uphold the highest levels of professionalism in their practice and should immediately alert the neuropsychologist if an ethical dilemma presents itself.

Ethical Standard 2: Competence—The sub-standards of Ethical Standard 2 focus on working within our bounds of competence. We agree to only work within the bounds of the competencies we have attained to date and to be honest about our level of expertise. In cases where new services are needed, we agree to gain adequate training and supervision to build competence. For psychometrists, this means only administering and scoring assessments that they have been formally trained on, and not agreeing to complete assessments for which they are unqualified or untrained. We agree to maintain competence through ongoing training, and the training we seek is based on scientific and professional knowledge in the field. The final two sub-standards pertain to only delegating work to those who are adequately trained to complete said work, and to refrain from taking on work if a personal problem will prevent the psychologist from doing their work in a competent manner.

Ethical Standard 3: Human Relations—The sub-standards of Ethical Standard 3 state that we do not discriminate, harass, demean, or torture others. We avoid harm at all costs and, in so doing, do not knowingly enter into a multiple relationship if there is the chance of harm or exploitation. We avoid conflicts of interest and do not exploit others due to our position of authority. When we are hired to provide services through a third party, we clarify roles, discuss the nature of the relationship of all parties and the intended use of the information gathered, outline fees, and review limits to confidentiality at the outset. We cooperate with other professionals when it is in the best interest of our clients. Should we deliver services to or through an organization, we again clarify roles, outline objectives of the service and the intended use of the information, discuss the relationship between all parties, access rights to the information, and limitations to confidentiality. For all services, we obtain informed consent from the individual or individuals receiving services. Language used is reasonably understandable and, in cases where an individual is incapable of providing consent, assent is obtained by the individual and consent signed by the legal guardian or party. We work to protect all individuals' rights and welfare, and consider the individuals preferences and best interests. Finally, we make reasonable steps to plan for unexpected interruptions in service provision, such as illness, retirement or death.

Ethical Standard 4: Privacy and Confidentiality—Sub-standards in Ethical Standard 4 discuss the importance of maintaining the privacy and confidentiality of our clients. Not only do we protect confidential information, we discuss the limits to confidentiality and the use of the information we obtain at the outset of services. Should audio or video recording be used, we obtain written permission, and we make clear the limitations of confidentiality if information is shared via electronic means (e.g., email). If we seek professional consultation with another provider, or we choose to use information gained from our clients for didactics, public media, or otherwise, we do not disclose personally identifiable information or any information that could reasonably lead to identification of the client. When gathering information from the client, we only include information in our reports that is germane to the purpose of the communication, and maintain the privacy and confidentiality of that information shared that is sensitive and unnecessary to include. Should there be a need to disclose confidential information, consent is obtained unless mandated by law.

Ethical Standard 5: Advertising and Other Public Statements—The sub-standards in Ethical Standard 5 discuss the sharing of information via advertisement or other public means. We do not knowingly make statements, share information, print information, or disseminate information that is false, deceptive or fraudulent concerning our work. Even if others make statements on our behalf, we retain the professional responsibility for those claims. When making public statements or sharing advice via the Internet, in print, or otherwise, the information shared is based on professional knowledge, training or experience, is consistent with the ethics code, and it is made clear that the statements made do not constitute the entry into a professional relationship with the recipient. Should we engage in a workshop or educational program, information shared is accurately described and all relevant information (audience, objectives, fees, etc.) is included. We claim our credentials only if they are granted from a regionally accredited educational institution or were the basis for licensure in our state. Finally, we do not solicit testimonials from current clients (that could be considered undue influence), and we do not engage in uninvited solicitation of business from clients unless it is for the benefit of helping an already engaged client, or is a component of disaster or community outreach service.

Ethical Standard 6: Record Keeping and Fees—The sub-standards of Ethical Standard 6 revolve around maintenance of records and fees for services rendered. We agree to maintain accurate and detailed records of our clients and they remain under our control to store, retain and dispose of records in compliance with the expectations of the law. We maintain confidentiality in this record keeping and use coding or other unique identifiers if information is entered into databases or otherwise available to those who were not granted consent by the client. We make plans to transfer records while maintaining confidentiality in the event of retirement or other withdrawal from practice. We also are forbidden from withholding records from requesting parties due to client non-payment. Fees are outlined and agreed upon at the earliest point feasible in the professional relationship. If limitations to services are expected given an inability to pay the full fee, this is also discussed at the outset. Should a client not pay for services, a collection agency or other retrieval service may be used, but only after informing the client and informing him/her of the measures that will be taken to obtain owed fees. Bartering with clients for services rendered is acceptable as long as it is not exploitative or clinically contraindicated. Any reporting of information provided to payors for services is made accurately. Finally, should any fee be divided with another professional, fee payment is based on services rendered by each professional, not based on the referral itself.

Ethical Standard 7: Educational Training—Many of the sub-standards under Ethical Standard 7 do not directly apply to psychometrists. Broadly, these sub-standards discuss education and training programs, information taught, and the requirements of students in these programs. The one sub-standard that is worth mentioning is expectations around assessing student and/or supervisee performance. We agree to establish a timely and routine process for both evaluating and subsequently providing feedback to our students and trainees. As psychometrists are working under the psychologists' supervision, it is expected that psychologists evaluate the psychometrists performance in a routine and timely manner and that the evaluation is based on the psychometrist's performance, similar to a performance review. Finally, we agree not to engage in sexual relationships with our students, psychometrists, or trainees.

Ethical Standard 8: Research and Publication—Once again, the sub-standards under Ethical Standard 8 do not directly pertain to the provision of psychometric services. They discuss the importance of gaining institutional approval for research studies, the informed consent process for both participation and audio/video recording and the importance of protecting the welfare of research participants. These sub-standards review instances when informed consent is unnecessary, as well as the importance to avoid inducements or deception in research procedures. When deception is unavoidable, debriefing should be provided as soon as feasible. The ethical use and care for animals used in research is reviewed. The final sub-standards discuss the importance of accuracy when reporting data, and forbids data fabrication, plagiarism, or the republishing of previously published data. Credit for work completed in publication is outlined, and should a psychologist be asked to review a study or publication, the confidentiality of proprietary information is maintained. Psychologists also agree to disseminate data on which their research publications are based for replication, reanalysis, or otherwise.

Ethical Standard 9: Assessment—As one might expect, there are a few sub-standards under Ethical Standard 9 that directly pertain to psychometrists and their work, as these sub-standards pertain specifically to assessment. Arguably, the most important standard for psychometrists is 9.02a: Use of Assessments. It states:

> (a) Psychologists administer, adapt, score, interpret, or use assessment techniques, interviews, tests, or instruments in a manner and for purposes that are appropriate in light of the research on or evidence of the usefulness and proper application of the techniques.

Parts B and C discuss using reliable and valid measures, and choosing measures that are in an appropriate language for the client. Of equal importance to the practice of psychometry is 9.11: Maintaining Test Security. It states:

> The term *test materials* refers to manuals, instruments, protocols, and test questions or stimuli and does not include *test data* as defined in Standard 9.04, Release of Test Data. Psychologists make reasonable efforts to maintain the integrity and security of test materials and other assessment techniques consistent with law and contractual obligations, and in a manner that permits adherence to this Ethics Code.

Additional sub-standards in this section pertain more to psychologists. Specifically, we obtain informed consent and do not release test data without written consent of the client or his/her guardian. Other sub-standards relate to the creation of test measures, the inclusion of particular data regarding tests in reports, our interpretation and subsequent explanation of assessment data to clients. We agree not to use obsolete or outdated tests, nor to hire or permit unqualified individual to access or engage in assessment without adequate training and appropriate supervision.

Ethical Standard 10: Therapy—The final set of standards pertains to the provision of therapeutic services, which is outside of the bounds of competence of psychometrists. As I am aware of some institutions that train psychometrists to administer therapy protocols in the context of a research study, I will briefly review the way these standards would pertain to individuals serving in this capacity. We agree to obtain informed consent and to be explicit in the contents of our informed consent forms. When there is multiple parties (e.g., couples, groups, individuals already under the care of a licensed psychologist), clarity around roles, discussions about treatment issues, and limits to confidentiality are discussed at the outset of services. Sexual relations with current or former clients, family members or relatives is forbidden. We agree not to accept our past sexual partners as current therapy clients. Finally, if unforeseen interruption in therapeutic services occurs, we make reasonable efforts to resolve any needs, keeping the welfare of the client in mind. We also terminate therapy when it is no longer clinically indicated, or if we are threatened while providing services.

As noted earlier, neuropsychologists should provide a copy of state statutes and relevant state-specific information to their psychometrist. I wholeheartedly believe psychometrists are bound by the same ethical and professional codes that we are as neuropsychologists, as they are working as a direct extension of our licenses.

Ongoing Conversations

The conversation about ethics does not stop after training as a psychometrist. Particularly for psychometrists in a larger group practice or affiliated with an academic medical institution, quarterly ethics meetings or professional seminars should be dedicated to reviewing ethical guidelines. Psychometrists should be encouraged to seek out their supervising neuropsychologist any time they feel uncomfortable or want to quickly consult about an ethical issue.

As neuropsychologists, our reaction to ethical conversations will dictate the willingness or likelihood that our psychometrists will come back to speak with us about concerns in the future. Taking a supportive, listening stance first (e.g., "tell me your concern and why you feel there is a questionable ethics component") and then attempting to join with the psychometrist (e.g., "I am so glad you brought this to my attention, let's talk about how I (or we) will handle it.") as part of an ongoing teachable moment can help your psychometrist feel listened to, supported, and understood. It will also increase the likelihood that they will bring concerns up again if they arise in the future.

Maintaining Our Own Ethical Boundaries

As with many other chapters in this book, survey responses helped me understand examples of ethical dilemmas faced by psychometrists in practice. For example, some psychometrists detailed times where they were asked to conduct family interviews, write sections of the report, or act outside of their bounds of competence. As discussed in Chapter 3, details around what they psychometrists' duties are, and what they are not, should not be left to interpretation. Understanding the power differential between psychometrist and neuropsychologist means that the onus of responsibility once again falls to the neuropsychologist to ask the psychometrist to engage in only those tasks within their bounds of competence or as outlined in their job responsibilities. We simply must practice within the highest ethical standards each day.

Results of the surveys collected for this book most frequently noted the biggest transgression of neuropsychologists was when they ask psychometrists to write sections of the report or to administer testing they had never seen or reviewed before. More concerning were those (albeit rare) survey responses that indicated that psychometrists were being asked to conduct patient interviews, provide patient feedback, review forensic case records and write a history, or draft the entirety of a report for clients. My hope is that, while the surveys discussing these practices were anonymous, individuals reading this book will agree that these requests are highly inappropriate and borderline unethical, and should not continue. Other dilemmas faced by psychometrists included requests to test patients while the neuropsychologist was not on-site, or requests to complete tasks that felt more menial and devaluing (e.g., purchasing lunch, picking up dry cleaning). While these latter two requests may not occur as frequently in a larger academic setting, private practitioners are encouraged to consider the appropriateness of these requests of their staff people.

References

American Psychological Association. (2017). *Ethical Principles of Psychologists and Code of Conduct* (2002, amended effective June 1, 2010 and January 1, 2017). Retrieved from: www.apa.org/ethics/code.

Brickman, A.M., Cabo, R., & Manly, J.J. (2006). Ethical issues in cross-cultural neuropsychology. *Applied Neuropsychology*, *13*(2), 91–100.

7 A Theoretical Framework for Training Psychometrists

"A profession without a model commands no respect."—Linas Bieliauskas (p. 23; Bieliauskas, 2008)

As touched upon in Chapter 2, in 1989, the Division 40 Task Force on Education, Accreditation, and Credentialing (hereafter referred to as "the Task Force") issued recommendations for education and training of non-doctoral personnel in the field of neuropsychology (Division 40 Task Force on Education, Accreditation, and Credentialing, 1989). First, authors acknowledge that many neuropsychologists may prefer to perform their own assessment batteries. However, for those who wish to employ non-doctoral personnel, the article moves on to discuss the wide acceptance of the use of these individuals in the field, and the specific role the psychometrist plays in the comprehensive neuropsychological evaluation process. It states that "technicians have a very narrowly defined and highly specific role in the overall process" (p. 24; Division 40 Task Force on Education, Accreditation, and Credentialing, 1989), which only includes administration and scoring of tests under the supervision of a licensed neuropsychologist. All other aspects of the evaluation, including interviews, test selection, interpretation, and communication of results are "*the sole and exclusive responsibility of the licensed neuropsychologist.*" (p. 24, emphasis added; Division 40 Task Force on Education, Accreditation, and Credentialing, 1989). It further mentions that "senior" or more advanced psychometrists may be involved in the training of new psychometrists, though the onus of responsibility for training procedures and assurance of competence remains with the neuropsychologist.

While these publications set the stage for the use of psychometrists in the field, over 30 years later, no specific model or framework has yet been published outlining minimum standards of competence or a proposed structure for psychometrists' training. After conducting a review of the literature, it appears that Bloom's taxonomy is a frequently used framework for organizing training procedures, and one that fits well with the training objectives of psychometry.

DOI: 10.4324/9781003098010-8

Bloom's taxonomy is a theoretical framework often applied to systematizing and organizing curriculum and teaching objectives (Bloom et al., 1956). It has previously been applied to training in various types of assessment (e.g., Ramirez, 2017), and it is an appropriate model that takes into account trainees who may enter training at various stages of experience. The learning objective in Bloom's taxonomy builds hierarchically, moving from basic (recall) to complex (abstraction), deepening the level of understanding as the complexity of topics build. Bloom's six levels include the following:

1. **Knowledge**: knowledge of specific facts, terms, theories, information
2. **Comprehension**: understanding, paraphrasing, summarizing and providing examples
3. **Application**: use of skills that are applied to varying situations
4. **Analysis**: analysis of elements and relationships
5. **Synthesis**: generation of data
6. **Evaluation**: critical thinking, extrapolation

The following is a proposed theoretical framework for training psychometrists, with sample measurable benchmarks to quantify training at various levels.

Training Level I: Knowledge—Review of Manuals and Written Materials

As the base level of learning, knowledge addresses the psychological processes of remembering or recalling information. It assumes little to no pre-existing knowledge and is enhanced through repetition. When applying this framework to psychometrist training, the focus is on an extensive review of testing manuals, introduction to different types of testing and domains of functioning assessed, and review of specific directions and standardized procedures.

Early goals and objectives for psychometrist training could include:

- Recognizing the names of tests
- State what a particular test measures
- Recite memorized introduction to or directions for a specific task
- State the age range of a particular test or the approximate length of administration time
- Name tests that assess a particular domain
- Identify stimulus books and materials for a given task

Training Level II: Comprehension—Shadowing and Observation

At the level of comprehension, psychometrists already understand assessments and can explain them in their own words. Training progresses from theoretical discussions to in vivo observation, as the psychometrist begins observing the neuropsychologist with his or her patients, or begins shadowing a more senior psychometrist in order to gain increased familiarity with testing procedures with current clients. Psychometrists may be encouraged to note and discuss behavioral observations during particular tasks. Psychometrists also observe scoring methods, including both hand scoring and computerized scoring of measures.

Goals and objectives for this next level of training could include:

- Paraphrase test directions and give a broad overview of task expectations
- Explain the use of a test and what domain it measures
- Provide examples of cases or scenarios when a test may be administered
- Identify whether a measure is scored by hand or with a computer, and describe the types of scores the test provides

Training Level III: Application—Administration, Practice, and Refinement

Moving from comprehension to application, psychometrists in training move from talking about testing to engaging in it. First, psychometrists may practice with their training neuropsychologist or with a senior psychometrist on staff. The psychometrist may then move on to test relatively high functioning individuals, progressing to increasingly challenging patients, all while under supervision and receiving ample feedback.

Goals and objectives for this level of training could include:

- Practice administration of an assessment to a neuropsychologist
- Administer a block of tests to a senior psychometrist
- Administer one assessment to a patient with supervisor in the room
- Administer a block of assessments and receive constructive feedback

Training Level IV: Analysis—Score Compilation and Data Generation

Once comfortable administering diverse assessments to clients, the focus of training transitions to scoring and score table generation. Aspects of training around scoring include conceptual understanding as to how scores are generated and classified, as well as instances where specific scales may comprise a composite score.

Goals and objectives for this level of training could include:

- Tally raw score totals
- Determine appropriate normative data sample
- Identify raw score conversion to standard score, T score, and so forth for client

- Score assessments by hand to understand how scores are generated
- Enter raw scores into computerized scoring programs for ease of increased efficiency

Training Level V: Synthesis—Generalization and the "Why"

After administering an assessment successfully, psychometrists at this level of training are encouraged to begin considering the "why" of the evaluation. Gaining the knowledge of why a measure is administered and what the neuropsychologist is looking to measure when administering a particular task deepens the psychometrist's understanding of testing more broadly, and often enhances the detail provided when later reviewing behavioral observations during specific tasks.

Goals and objectives for this level of training could include:

- Describe why a particular measure is given as part of a comprehensive neuropsychological battery
- Identify diverse behaviors likely to be observed during a particular task
- Discuss behaviors that might be observed if an individual has a deficit in the domain being assessed
- Group similar types of tests based on the domain they measure (e.g., verbal memory tasks)

Training Level VI: Evaluation and Maintenance of Competence

At this final level of training, psychometrists are encouraged to think critically about the measures they administer. Ongoing conversations with their attending neuropsychologist deepen their understanding of how batteries are constructed and why certain measures are given. For example, a psychometrist who understands that fine motor weaknesses can impact drawing on a visual memory task may engage with their attending neuropsychologist to discuss switching to a visual memory task with reduced motor demands.

Goals and objectives for this level of training could include:

- Compare and contrast two different measures of sustained attention
- Discuss strengths and weaknesses of a particular measure
- Identify patients or populations for which a measure may be inappropriate to administer
- Identify instances when testing of limits may be appropriate with a client
- Review new measures recently published and discuss pros and cons of their use with different populations

While some may find that the taxonomy model described earlier fits nicely with their methods of training, as I discussed in Chapter 1, there is also a large competency-model push within the psychology. Here is a quick review of a second model or structure for training. It is likely that as the competency model is one from which supplemental training goals and benchmarks can be pulled.

Competency: The "Cube Model"

As discussed in Chapter 1, identifying core professional competences and defining and measuring learning outcomes has been a focus of increasing attention for professional psychology. The APA-sponsored 2002 Competence Conference: Future Directions in Education and Credentialing aimed to clarify issues raised in the identification, education and training, and assessment of competencies within professional psychology (Kaslow, 2004; Kaslow et al., 2004). The "cube model" of core competency areas in psychology was a result of the 2002 Competencies Conference (Rodolfa et al., 2005). It identifies 12 core competencies across foundational (*x*-axis) or functional (*y*-axis) domains that are expected to be gained over the course of a psychologist's training (*z*-axis). This cube model has been applied to competency benchmarks in clinical health psychology (France et al., 2008), rehabilitation psychology (Hibbard & Cox, 2010) and more recently to clinical neuropsychology (Rey-Casserly et al., 2012). Revisions to the initial competencies outlined by Rey-Casserly and colleagues were later published as the result of a task force review by members of the CNS (Smith & CNS, 2019).

While the competency model outlined by Smith and the CNS extend far beyond the expected competencies of a psychometrist, it is appropriate to acknowledge the overlapping necessity to provide foundational training in areas such as ethics, individual and cultural diversity, reflective practice/self-care/self-assessment, professional identity, and relationships, which are integrated into multiple chapters of this text. Further, it provides a model for assessing competence across diverse competencies in psychometry (see Appendix for Psychometrist Competence and Skill Evaluation Form for created based on this model). As we as a field strive to identify competencies for neuropsychologists, we must also consider the competency of those we hire who administer testing to the patients we serve.

References

Bieliauskas, L.A. (2008). The preparation of the clinical neuropsychologist: Contemporary training models and specialization. *Textbook of Clinical Neuropsychology*, 18–24.

Bloom, B. (Ed.), Englehart, M.D., Furst, E.J., Hill, W.H., & Krathwohl, D.R. (1956). *Taxonomy of Educational Objectives: Handbook 1. Cognitive Domain*. White Plains, NY: Longman.

Division 40 Task Force on Education, Accreditation, and Credentialing. (1989). Guidelines regarding the use of nondoctoral personnel in clinical neuropsychological assessment. *The Clinical Neuropsychologist*, *3*(1), 23–24.

France, C.R., Masters, K.S., Belar, C.D., Kerns, R.D., Klonoff, E.A., Larkin, K.T., . . . Thorn, B.E. (2008). Application of the competency model to clinical health psychology. *Professional Psychology: Research and Practice*, *39*, 573–580.

Hibbard, M.R., & Cox, D.R. (2010). Competencies of a rehabilitation psychologist. In R.G. Frank, M. Rosenthal & B. Caplan (Eds.), *Handbook of Rehabilitation Psychology* (2nd Ed., pp. 467–475). Washington, DC: American Psychological Association.

Kaslow, N.J. (2004). Competencies in professional psychology. *American Psychologist*, *59*, 774–781.

Kaslow, N.J., Borden, K.A., Collins Jr., F.L., Forrest, L., Illfelder-Kaye, J., Nelson, P.D., . . . Wilmuth, M.E. (2004). Competencies conference: Future directions in education and credentialing in professional psychology. *Journal of Clinical Psychology*, *60*, 699–712.

Ramirez, T.V. (2017). On pedagogy of personality assessment: Application of Bloom's taxonomy of educational objectives. *Journal of Personality Assessment*, *99*(2), 146–152.

Rey-Casserly, C., Roper, B.L., & Bauer, R.M. (2012). Application of a competency model to clinical neuropsychology. *Professional Psychology: Research and Practice*, *43*(5), 422–431.

Rodolfa, E., Bent, R., Eisman, E., Nelson, P., Rehm, L., & Ritchie, P. (2005). A cube model for competency development: Implications for psychology educators and regulators. *Professional Psychology: Research and Practice*, *36*, 347–354.

Smith, G., & CNS. (2019). Education and training in clinical neuropsychology: Recent developments and documents from the clinical neuropsychology synarchy. *Archives of Clinical Neuropsychology*, *34*(3), 418–431.

8 A Practical Guide to Training Psychometrists

Part I: Welcome, Assessment of Knowledge, and Key Readings

When your psychometrist walks in the door, your initial instinct may be to have him or her jump straight in to observing the testing. While this may be appropriate for some psychometrists or certain situations, I am going to frame this chapter in the context of a brand new psychometrist who has never worked as a psychometrist before. It is assumed this new trainee has not had significant training beyond the possibility of a few undergraduate courses and perhaps some experience working with others (e.g., day care, food service, camp counselor). Therefore, priming the trainee with some initial readings and conversations around topics like ethics, confidentiality, and test security provides the foundation from which the psychometrist will grow.

The best way I've found to structure training is to allow the psychometrist to share a bit about their experience before we get started. This may have been covered in your initial interview (see the Appendix for my Psychometrist Candidate Interview Form), but this is a great time to learn more about their experience working with others and about any familiarity or experience they have with formal tests. For example, a psychometrist who worked in a day-care or after-school care facility likely has behavior management experience. Similarly, those who have worked in the food service industry likely have good customer service and rapport-building skills. Given the lack of formal psychometry training programs, connecting aspects of training to their prior experiences, when possible, will make learning that much more meaningful.

Welcome to the Practice, Clinic, or Department

Training begins with a broad overview of the practice, a discussion around different members of the practice or department with whom the psychometrist will work, and a comprehensive overview of job expectations, roles, and boundaries (*see* Chapters 3 and 15).

DOI: 10.4324/9781003098010-9

Assessment of Skills and Competencies

For those psychometrists with any background in the subject, provide them with a list of the tests in your practice and ask them to rank their familiarity and experience with each one. Leave space for them to write in any supplemental tests that they have administered (*see* Assessment of Psychometrist's Testing Experience in the Appendix). While familiarity does not change the training process significantly, if I know they have given a similar type of test when reviewing one from my battery, I can link their prior knowledge to the learning of this new test.

The Reading List

Once we review the practice, discuss prior experience, and assess various test knowledge, I provide a list of required readings that includes citations for relevant readings in ethics/confidentiality (*see* Chapter 6), a summary of the standards that detail the rights of test takers (*see* Chapter 5), and the pertinent sections from the APA Guidelines for Test User Qualifications (discussed later). I also provide a full copy of the APA Ethics Code, state statutes, Standards, and APA Test User Qualification articles, though it is not required that a psychometrist read these texts in their entirety.

I also provide specific readings around behavioral observations (*see* Chapter 12) and cultural competence/diverse populations (*see* Chapter 14), though I also spend time, typically on the second day of training, reviewing my behavioral observation checklist and discussing cultural competence more broadly. I remind the psychometrist that this is an introduction, that areas such as ethics, cultural competence, and working with diverse populations will come up frequently in our supervision and professional development meetings, and that discussion regarding these topics is always welcome.

Part II: Training in Test Administration

The APA Guidelines for Test User Qualifications (Turner et al., 2001) outlines comprehensive guidelines for test users. These were written to inform test users and the general public about the qualifications that APA finds important for the competent and responsible use of psychological tests. Therefore, as we dive into the process of training in test use and administration, let's start with a key definition:

> **Test user qualification:** "the combination of knowledge, skills, abilities, training, experience, and, where appropriate, practice credentials that the APA considers desirable for the responsible use of psychological test."
>
> (p. 1099; Turner et al., 2001)

While, like many other documents, the APA assumes the individual administering the test is also interpreting the results and providing feedback (completing the full assessment process), there are certain key skills and areas of knowledge recommended for review that are pertinent to the work of psychometrists (p. 1103; Turner et al., 2001):

- Legal rights of test takers
- Standardized administration procedures
- Confidentiality of test materials and test information
- Safeguards for protecting test material (protection against copyright infringement, protection against unauthorized dissemination of test items, keys, and scoring procedures)
- Safeguards for protecting protocols and test results (legal and ethical issues)

Typically, all of the aforementioned bullet points have already been reviewed if the psychometrist has read the required readings around ethics and standardization. Thus, we are quickly able to transition into the "meat and potatoes" of training: test administration and scoring.

Manual Review

I spend a good couple of hours walking through a manual (or several) with the psychometrist (*see* Sample Test Review Form in the Appendix) to start. This form provides a framework for the review of each test, allowing the psychometrist to pull pertinent information as the manual is reviewed. Often, these sheets are included in their training binder and can be tailored to the practice of that neuropsychologist (since not all neuropsychologists have the same test lists or battery approaches). As new tests are reviewed, additional pages are added to the psychometrist's binder. In this way, if there are measures that are administered less frequently, the psychometrist has a quick reference they can refer to, as needed. While more senior psychometrists could just photocopy these forms for newer psychometrists, I find it to be a helpful exercise for inexperienced trainees to create the forms themselves. The process certainly accelerates with practice, and it is a nice way to ensure everyone is interpreting the manual in a similar way.

Shadow/Observe (Preferably Multiple Individuals)

Depending on the number of neuropsychologists or senior psychometrists in your practice or department, it is of benefit to the new trainee to sit in and observe as many different individuals administering tests as possible. Ideally, this assumes regular recalibration efforts so that the psychometrist is observing the same administration practice despite different testers. It can benefit the new trainee to take notes in order to have something to review with the test administrators at the end of the day. The psychometrist should be encouraged to take notes both about the neuropsychologist/senior psychometrist's administration and about any relevant client behaviors. I try to check in with the psychometrist over lunch and then at the end of the testing day in order to review notes, discuss observations, and answer questions that arise.

In smaller practices or where feasible, it may be beneficial to pair one psychometrist with one neuropsychologist to start in order to allow the trainee to fully understand their supervising neuropsychologist's preferences, needs, and expectations.

Note that the observation period starts long before the client walks into the room for testing. I ask the psychometrist to join me while I collect necessary materials, pull testing forms, sharpen pencils, and set up the room. I also talk with them about my order of administration, the rationale behind why I place some tests before others (e.g., why certain verbal naming tests are not to be administered in the delay of verbal memory tasks), and what my expectations are around behaviors to look out for or things to consider during testing. At the end of the day, we meet to go over the entire battery, discuss each test administered, answer any questions that arise, and put away all the materials so they are ready for the next day. I don't have the psychometrist join me for scoring until they are a few days into training, but as with this entire training process, that is completely up to your personal preferences.

Mock Administrations (Increasingly Challenging Patients)

Mock administrations are described as one of the most helpful experiences for new psychometrists in training. Silently reading the words written in the manual is one thing, but actually saying them aloud, coordinating the statements with either the handing of materials to the client or the pointing to of specific things, all the while maintaining one's place in the direction set and observing the client for notable behaviors is a lot. Therefore, I tend to (1) administer at least some of the tests to the psychometrist so they can get a feel for how the client experiences the testing process (pointing out tips and tricks along the way), (2) have the psychometrist administer the test to me, again providing helpful hints, as needed, and then (3) later re-administer the test to me, but this second time I may throw in an unexpected response to help the psychometrist plan for the various responses of our clients. If there are senior psychometrists, increasing the opportunity for mock administrations can only help. I have seen some wonderfully creative responses by senior psychometrists that assist the new trainee with getting comfortable with the unexpected.

A note about mock administrations: many survey respondents said they appreciated the opportunity to bring tests home and practice on family members. While I understand the benefit of practice, and am aware that this is also common practice in graduate programs, I would encourage critical thinking around this option. For example, should the psychometrist's family member ever then need neuropsychological testing, they then have familiarity with some of the tests. Further, it is hard to guarantee test security in these instances. Therefore, caution is warranted in encouraging this option in your practice or department. If there are externs, interns, or other individuals in training, I believe these individuals would be more than happy to support a psychometrist in training—and more appropriate choices.

Administer With Support

It tends to be most helpful if the psychometrist can begin by administering one or two tests to a patient when first starting out. This allows the individual to get a sense of testing, preferably on a measure they feel quite comfortable with but does not come with the added pressure of planning and subsequently administering an entire battery. As we know, administering one or two tests feels very different than taking a battery, choosing the order of administration, and juggling the many competing demands and pieces of the testing process.

As the psychometrist gains comfort, additional tests can be added. It is hard to predict how long this process can take, as it is highly dependent on the comfort, confidence, and competence of your psychometrist. Some psychometrists prefer multiple administrations with clients before adding on, while others will quickly move to administer as many tests as possible in rapid succession.

Administer Independently and Check Off

Once the psychometrist is comfortable with the full battery, I recommend sitting in on at least three full administrations. I tend to start with a behaviorally "easy" client and then schedule the psychometrist with clients who may present with increasingly challenging behaviors. Multiple observations of full batteries benefit both the psychometrist and the client alike, as it provides opportunity for rich discussion, allows for opportunities for "on the job" teachable moments, and gives the psychometrist time to get comfortable with the entire testing process. Once checked off, observations every six months are recommended (*see* Test Administration Check Off sheet in the Appendix).

Part III: Training in Scoring

As mentioned previously, I don't immediately jump into training in scoring procedures with my psychometrists on day one of observation, though I also don't wait until they are fully competent and testing independently. I believe there is a lot to learn from an administration and behavioral observation standpoint, and thus I would much prefer to wait on adding yet another process to their learning list until they feel at least somewhat comfortable with aspects of the testing process. Typically, discussions around scoring start after their second or third observation. This may not be an option in some clinics or practices, and there is no reason a psychometrist *can't* learn the scoring with administration—I just personally find it preferable in my practice. Therefore, consider this section as somewhat occurring in tandem with Part II.

Similar to the iterative approach to training in test administration, I start by having the psychometrist observe me scoring. Analogous to a sportscaster, I talk aloud the entire time, showing them things of note or talking about ways that certain subscales are derived, for example. I also train my psychometrist to hand score tests before they are introduced to the beautiful world of computer scoring. In this way, they get a better sense of how scores are tabulated. Once again, this may not be your preference, but I find it assists with a deeper understanding of the scoring process down the road. We then co-score, or the psychometrist scores and I watch or double-check it thereafter. Periodically, I pull a file (approximately every three to six months) and rescore it in its entirety, again to be sure skills do not drift.

As discussed previously, psychometrists in my practice receive a training binder when they first arrive. Into this binder goes their administration sheets, any cheat sheets I've created (or that they create for themselves), notes, pertinent readings, and a whole lot of other forms I've created to support their ongoing training. I nonetheless encourage the psychometrist to create their own scoring binder, as having all the normative tables in one spot allows for a more efficient scoring process at the end of the day. Somewhat tedious initially, I find this can save significant time in the long run.

I also provide the psychometrist with a score table template. This template has all of the tests I use, with the relevant subscales listed. It has columns for raw score, standard score, percentile, and descriptor (*see* Score Table in the Appendix). Once proficient in scoring, we review the process of score transformation, and the psychometrist begins to create score tables. While I do not include a chapter on basic statistics in this book, I include a handout with the formulas for basic score conversions that I also include as part of each psychometrist's training manual (*see* Score Conversion Handout in the Appendix).

Part IV: Training in Behavior Management and Behavioral Observation

While training in behavioral observation is also largely in tandem with observation, I want to highlight a few key points in the training process (*see* Chapter 11 for a lengthy discussion of behavioral observations). Most survey respondents endorsed using some sort of checklist or formal behavioral observation sheet for training. If a psychometrist observes me testing, I then walk through the entire behavioral observation sheet, reviewing pertinent observations the psychometrist made and adding my own notes to supplement.

We also review any behavioral management strategies the psychometrist observes me use during sessions. We discuss my introductory remarks, and how the psychometrist can introduce themselves to the client (*see* Chapter 11 for sample methods of introduction and ways to respond to certain behaviors in testing). I also reiterate the importance of alerting me immediately for (1) known or suspected abuse or neglect, (2) suicidal or homicidal ideation or intent, or (3) any aggressive, harassing, or threatening comments or behaviors. I remind the psychometrist that while we are providing a professional service, safety of ourselves and the clients we serve is paramount. Thus, if there is any threat or harassing remark made, exit the room and find me immediately.

Final Discussion Points

Before a client arrives at your office or clinic, it is important to review the "flow" of the evaluation process with your psychometrist. Often they have an understanding of this from observing, but passively seeing and actively doing are entirely different experiences. Perhaps you have a dedicated block of time at the end of the day to review the test list for the next day's case, discuss any relevant background history, and provide any insight into behaviors to be on the lookout for. Perhaps there is a meeting every Friday where all the cases and test lists for the upcoming week are reviewed. Whatever your preference, structuring the process benefits you, the client, and your psychometrist.

It can also be beneficial to use check sheets or progress sheets to document the client's flow through the testing procedure. This can include a place to keep track of dates of interview, testing, scoring, table creation, file provision to the neuropsychologist, file return to the psychometrist, report provision to the client, feedback session, file scanning, and chart closure. While I used to keep a paper form, I have recently updated to using a shared HIPAA secure document, as this allows all staff to access it and keep it updated simultaneously.

Current Neuropsychologists and Psychometrists' General Tips and Tricks for Training

The survey respondents shared many supportive tips and tricks; the following list is a representative sample.

From Psychometrists

- Speak to your psychometrist from day one about their position and how they fit into the department. Help them to understand your expectations and how they can grow within their role.
- Have your psychometrist observe you both before *and after* they begin testing. Although initial observations are helpful, observing after testing several people is even more helpful because testing raises questions that a psychometrist may not have thought of before.
- Observe your psychometrist even after they are comfortable testing. We all drift, and it is good to catch it before it gets out of hand.
- Give constructive criticism, emphasis on *constructive*. You've been doing this a lot longer; they'll eventually get the hang of it, and they need your help to get there.
- Be open to the feedback of psychometrists when they are having difficulty continuing testing with a patient. They are in the room, so if they come to talk to you about concerns, be open to their experience and feedback.
- Set aside time each week to touch base with your psychometrist, especially in the early months of training. Stay in close contact during evaluations, as sometimes questions or problems arise quickly.
- When possible, train your psychometrist specifically in the ways of your assessment process. The trust between psychometrist and neuropsychologist is really important, and the more the psychometrist understands your "why," the more they can provide you with good information.
- Beyond training in testing and scoring, train your psychometrist in how to deal with the emotions that arise during testing. Sometimes they come out of nowhere, and it can be challenging to navigate if you are not prepared.
- Psychometrists are not computers or work horses. Your data are only as good as your psychometrist, and your psychometrist is only as good as the training, resources, and support you provide them.
- Get to know your psychometrist a bit before training. Many of the psychometrists I work with come from diverse backgrounds, and thus all of our training needs to be tailored to our differences.
- Emphasize the importance of being proactive. During testing, your psychometrist should be thinking 10–15 minutes ahead of time.
- Don't underestimate the frequency of simple addition errors. Encourage score checking, particularly after a notably challenging patient.
- Don't be afraid to start a conversation with "Are you familiar with this?" Sometimes, psychometrists know more about a topic than expected, but then wish there was more time spent on other topics. Try to be open to feedback around areas of interest in the training process.

From Fellow Neuropsychologists

Give your psychometrist praise and attention! They are working very hard on your behalf.

Realize the training process will take many more months than you initially anticipated. Remember it is your license on the line, so take the time and put in the effort.

Do not rush the training. Bad habits are hard to fix, so teach them the correct way from the start.

Check scoring randomly and continuously. Even after a psychometrist is deemed competent, randomly observe. Be sure you always remain on the same page with both scoring and administration.

Remember how many mistakes you made as a trainee, and normalize the likelihood that mistakes will arise. No one is perfect, and you want to foster open communication when mistakes happen.

Be direct in your expectations and share tips and tricks you've picked up along the way. Encourage questions and positively reinforce their interest and dedication to learning your methods.

Foster work–life balance to reduce burnout and ask for their feedback to build rapport and establish a team mentality.

Hire two psychometrists at a time so they can practice with each other.

Remember that your psychometrist is a direct reflection of your practice. Fostering both testing and interpersonal skills is crucial.

Have patience. Praise strengths. Listen. Teach. Learn.

Reference

Turner, S.M., DeMers, S.T., Fox, H.R., & Reed, G.M. (2001). APA's guidelines for test user qualifications: An executive summary. *American Psychologist, 56*(12), 1099–1113.

9 Preparation in Advance of the Client's Arrival

One of the most consistent themes of survey responses was the importance of advanced preparation. In the pages that follow, I review some of the most common ways to help your psychometrists to get organized and prepare for clients prior to their arrival.

Client Chart Review

Many neuropsychologists endorse providing specific information to their psychometrist before the client arrives. Specifically, most will provide relevant demographic information (e.g., the client's name, date of birth, age, race/ethnicity, gender, handedness), and some will also provide referring concerns or premorbid diagnoses. This information sharing can be achieved through a demographics "face sheet" for the file, a quick written blurb, or a meeting the day or two before the client arrives. This is also a great time to share the test list and check in with the psychometrist about their comfort with any atypical additions to your battery or less frequently administered tests.

There appears to be a lack of consensus around sharing diagnoses with psychometrists prior to testing. On the one hand, some argue it is helpful for the psychometrist to be more aware of particular behavioral patterns based on a client's confirmed or suspected diagnosis, while others argue that by providing only minimal information about the client, they reduce bias or a tendency to "look out for" corroborating evidence of a diagnosis.

I agree there are clear pros and cons to both, although I would put forth a few additional considerations. It may be worthwhile for those preferring not to share diagnoses, at a minimum, to share concerns for particular behaviors that may arise—for example, if the client's file suggests that the psychometrist may face significant disinhibition, poor frustration tolerance, or aggression. While specific diagnoses may not be wholly relevant to the testing, the advanced warning around potentially challenging behaviors allows the psychometrist to prepare accordingly.

DOI: 10.4324/9781003098010-10

Test List Preparation

Pulling test protocols prior to the client's arrival is routine across the board. Most suggest putting these forms in the order of administration to keep the pace of the assessment flowing naturally. For those tests with delays, many suggest writing the time on the top of the delayed protocol and tucking the form behind whatever test is most likely to fill that time delay requirement. That way, even if something unexpectedly causes the psychometrist to forget about the delay, there is a visual reminder of the approximate time the test is to be completed.

Certainly, this paper-stacking advice centers around those tests with paper forms or protocols. With the increasing use of tablets and other paperless devices, I find it is still beneficial to mark times on the test list itself and keep the tablet close by to monitor when the delay countdown turns green.

To the extent possible, gathering stimulus books and other testing materials prior to the client's arrival will only increase efficiency in the moment. I prefer to lay out all materials next to me and then stack them or return them to their rightful place during breaks, a delay, or otherwise. This provides a visual reminder of any tests that are still to be administered and reduces the need to lug all ten test kits back to the cabinets or storage area at the end.

I typically ask my psychometrist to create the file prior to client arrival, although there are many institutions that may have front-office staff to create the folder and auto-generate labels with the client's identifying information. While I wait to affix the identification labels until the client arrives to the office (saves a lot of time on the back end if the client does not show for his or her evaluation), the folder allows all the client's information to be stored in one place.

If the psychometrist is using electronic devices (e.g., tablets, computers), it is beneficial to set these tests up ahead of time as well. Often an on-screen profile can be created for the client, allowing the psychometrist to enter all identifying information about the client before they are seated across the table. If a profile can be generated in advance, it can save a few moments of time during the testing itself and allow the psychometrist more control over the pace of testing the following day. For those who create digital files in which scoring documents are saved, a digital client folder on the storage server can also be prepared in advance of the client's arrival.

To the extent necessary, it may be worthwhile for the psychometrist to double-check the age range for each test before the client arrives. For example, perhaps the Nelson Denny Reading Test is listed, but the client turns out to be in 8th grade; or the WMS-IV Adult is listed, but the client requires the Older Adult form. We are all human and can certainly make mistakes, so it can be a good additional step to have the psychometrist verify age ranges prior to the start with the client.

Supplemental Supplies

Okay, the client information is shared, the paper file is ready, the electronic file is ready, so now it is important to gather supplemental supplies, as needed. I tend to encourage psychometrists to pull stimulus books and other test materials (e.g., grooved pegboard) the morning of the client's arrival. This way, they can remain locked in a secure location until they are used. I encourage multiple sharpened pencils (some with and some without erasers), a stopwatch (preferably one that does not beep and does not require advance degrees to operate), colored pencils (for those who switch pencils during the RCFT administration), and other notable essentials for the client. Specifically, I often include a few blank sheets of paper, crayons, and a variety of stickers if I am seeing a pediatric client. Any "tools for your toolbox" that can be packed the day before can be lifesaving if needed in a pinch.

There are also often supplemental forms, such as consents, qualitative questionnaires, or otherwise, that can be pulled and prepared before the client arrives—perhaps you have a specific behavioral observation checklist that can be included in the file as well. Any way to organize on the front end will save time, energy, and frustration on the back end.

One additional note about supplies: the psychometrist should always be completing forms in pen. If a mistake is made, my psychometrists are asked to draw one single line through the error, write the corrected information, and initial it. In this way, records are kept clean and there are no concerns for scribbles or erased responses. This is particularly important for psychometrists who work with neuropsychologists conducting forensic evaluations.

Mental Preparation

Particularly in the early stages of psychometrist training, I encourage a mental walk-through of the day ahead. My psychometrist and I do this "walk" together for the first few cases they see independently. This can be accomplished either the night before or in the morning before the client arrives, but it is important to review the order of administration and verify things like appropriate timing given memory testing delays, the importance of administering verbal tasks outside of a verbal memory delay, appropriate spacing of performance validity testing, and so forth. As the psychometrist becomes more seasoned, this review becomes less necessary, and the psychometrist is much more able to adapt to changes that arise in the testing day.

Scoring Preparation

Before the client arrives, it can be helpful to open manuals to the proper scoring tables (based on age, for example) so that measures can be scored during breaks in testing or as they are administered. While this again takes practice and is not something I encourage for new psychometrists just starting out, it can again be a method to maximize efficiency and afford the neuropsychologist data on the client before the appointment is over. Anything that is scored can be reviewed during a break, allowing the neuropsychologist to review progress and determine if any changes to the battery are appropriate.

10 Structuring the Space to Optimize the Testing Environment and Results

Data collected during the assessment process is heavily influenced by the surroundings in which it is obtained. Considerations around room setup, items in the space, and possibilities for distraction require a full sensory overview of the testing environment. In this chapter, I review many opportunities for unwanted distraction or discomfort that can be minimized when structuring the testing space.

The Ideal: One Table and Two Chairs

The optimal testing environment is boring: nothing to see, nothing to hear, nothing to smell. Ideally, it would be a comfortably sized room (not too small as to feel cramped, but not too large to feel swallowed up) with a table and two chairs. I want to emphasize the fact that this is ideal and is likely not attainable in most settings. For example, psychometrists working on an inpatient unit face far more challenges around distractions in the environment and unstructured testing circumstances than those routinely seeing clients in an outpatient private practice setting. While I will focus on what may be available in an outpatient setting, many of these considerations can be generalized to an inpatient setting as well.

Depending on the age of your clients, different table and chair setups may be required. It is also possible that multiple sizes of tables and chairs may need to be on hand and quickly switched out based on the client. For example, many pediatric practices use height-adjustable tables and varying sizes of chairs to fit the child being assessed. A rolling chair at a large conference table is the perfect setup for chair relay races but will likely result in little formal testing being accomplished. Similarly, a small chair that wobbles or feels uneven can make an adult or geriatric client feel unsupported and concerned that the slightest move will result in a broken chair and a tumble to the floor. A sturdy table that does not move back and forth will thwart concerns or distractions when writing or drawing. As is customary in restaurants, an unneeded piece of cardboard or anything handy can be used to solidify the table.

DOI: 10.4324/9781003098010-11

Some adult clients do benefit from a chair with wheels, as it allows them to turn the chair when initially sitting down and to roll in closer to the table to view stimulus books and other materials. However, the vast majority of clients tends to benefit more from a chair without wheels. To the extent that you have the means and opportunity, a variety of tables and chairs are best.

What Can Be Seen: Wall Décor, Lighting, and the Dreaded Clock

My mother taught kindergarten for decades, and I vividly remember going to her classroom over the summer and beginning to pepper the walls with vibrant pictures and stimulating visuals. While it can be tempting, particularly in a pediatric setting, to post pictures and other décor, these items can result in distractions or in some cases inflation of scores. I recall interviewing at a practice where the doctor's office coordinated with an animal theme. There were pictures of animals designating each testing or therapy room and decorating the hallways. These pictures would unknowingly inflate the scores on a verbal fluency measure, as all the child had to do looking around the room is name the pictures they saw. Distractions are relevant to adults as well; a picture of a dog hanging in the testing space may remind the client of a recently deceased pet, causing unintended emotional provocation and difficulty to focus on the task at hand. Therefore, less is more when it comes to décor.

The testing space should be outfitted with adequate light, optimally with lighting that does not buzz (i.e., fluorescent bulbs) or can be adjusted to the client's needs. It can be helpful to have a standing lamp that can supplement existing lighting for those patients who request increased light.

Now, the dreaded wall clock. Anyone who has ever stared intently at the ever-so-slow moving clock above a professor's head during an interminable lecture can relate. While it is not news to you, our tests can be rather boring to those who are taking them. Therefore, consideration around where the clock is positioned (if a clock is hung at all) is warranted. A psychometrist might find a wall clock placed directly behind the client to be a welcome addition to the testing space, as it allows them to track progress without seeming rude when they glance at their phone or watch. However, just because it is behind a client does not mean they won't turn around to check the time, especially if it is not silent.

What Can Be Heard: Thin Walls, Buzzing Smart Watches, Bustling Hallways, and Outdoor Noises

Supplementing visual concerns discussed earlier, the sounds the clock can make are an unwelcome distraction to anyone with reasonably decent hearing and can be torturous to those suffering from hypersensitivity to noise. In addition, the sound of a clock can promote anxiety or unwanted feelings of angst in the testing space.

Working in a clinic with paper-thin walls, I quickly observed that my own productivity was hampered by the stories I unintentionally heard in offices nearby. If I couldn't get a report written given the noise, how could I expect a client to repeat eight digits forward? This one is an easy fix. I purchased my own white noise machine to drown out sounds while testing a patient. As an added bonus, I quickly came to realize that keeping the white noise machine on for the entirety of the day allowed me to stay focused on my work and out of the drama of the day in the clinic. While there are some clients who may find the white noise machine distracting, I often turn it onto a low setting prior to the client's arrival so that they are not specifically attuned to it when I move to turn it on.

In a parallel situation, a waiting room that is situated close to the testing room may allow parents the unintended opportunity to listen to their child's responses to questions. A well-placed noise machine just outside of the testing door can enhance privacy so that those passing by or seated outside cannot hear what is happening in the testing space.

While this next point is less about the psychometrist training and more about broad practice operations, I highly encourage the neuropsychologist in private practice to spend time in the allotted testing space prior to signing a lease. If there is a public speaking firm next door or a dance studio offering tap dancing classes below, or even if there are train tracks that run behind the building, these can become external distractors with which even the best and loudest of white noise machines simply cannot compete.

Similarly, a white noise machine inside a testing space is no match for the buzzing of a phone or smart watch. With the inevitable progression of technology, it is important to remind psychometrists that electronics must be placed on silent mode and all notifications should be silenced for the entire time they are working with a patient.

I have not forgotten about those neuropsychologists whose psychometrists test inpatient or are testing on a hallway of offices in a bustling medical setting. When I worked on an inpatient unit, I was fortunate to have a dedicated testing space on the unit for those patients who were able to leave their rooms. For those who remained bedridden, my first few minutes were spent simultaneously establishing rapport with the patient, clearing the tray table, and structuring as much space as possible. Particularly in pediatric settings where families are encouraged to bring in toys and many comforts from home, spending a few minutes moving these comforts temporally out of the testing space can increase productivity for the very short amount of testing time available.

What Can Be Touched: Materials on the Table

The psychometrist will need a place to put testing materials and would benefit from touchdown space to get organized. In a private practice or outpatient clinic, this can easily be a desk or table behind the testing table or close in reach of the psychometrist. Most logically, this table or space should be out of arms reach of the client, particularly a hyperactive or impulsive one. In both adult and pediatric settings, impulse control can be a concern, and thus keeping the table clear of all unnecessary materials is best. Even if a client is benefiting from a visual aid or visual schedule to keep them on track, it can be helpful to view the visual schedule together and then place it in sight, but out of reach, so it does not cause unwanted distraction.

The COVID-19 pandemic helped me to further identify items in both the waiting room and testing space that were unnecessary or distracting, such as stacks of untouched magazines or plush toys that are difficult to clean. Although the pandemic required adding extra hand sanitizer and plexiglass shields, very few items remain on the testing table. Even the plexiglass shield base became a squeaky distraction to a client who noticed that the base was not fully secured to the shield, and leaving a bottle of hand sanitizer within the reach of a young child will quickly result in a puddle on the table.

What Can Be Smelled: Eggs for Breakfast and Tuna for Lunch

We've all had that colleague or staff person who brings aromatic leftovers for lunch. To the extent that it is possible, choose a testing space that is far away from scents or midday kitchen chatter. I once worked in a practice where the ventilation system wafted delicious lunch smells from the business next door, but often this resulted in the heightening of my own hunger cues.

It is also worth noting that while scoring during lunch or taking a working lunch in one's office can enhance productivity, it may be worth designating a kitchen area where a psychometrist can enjoy their lunch, snack, or meal. Keeping food out of testing spaces reduces the likelihood of any issues that could arise (e.g., smell sensitivities, unintended allergic reactions).

Not all distracting scents are food specific. Perfumes, aromatherapy candles, and other natural and unnatural room deodorizers can affect a patient's ability to concentrate. It may be necessary to engage in a somewhat uncomfortable conversation with your psychometrist around the use of excessive perfume, aftershave, or cologne, as well as the appropriateness of air fresheners within his or her designated testing space. The patient with an extremely sensitive nose will wholeheartedly appreciate these efforts.

The Psychometrist's Place at the Table

The final piece of the testing setup is the position of the psychometrist in relation to the patient. It is important that the psychometrist sit closest to the door in case of emergency. Particularly with adult clients, frustration can occasionally escalate to a threat of something physical, and it is therefore important that the psychometrist is quickly able to exit the testing space. Further, with pediatric clients, it can absolutely be the case that a child would like to leave the testing room and run to a parent nearby, and therefore the psychometrist needs to maintain control and ensure the client's safety by keeping the child in the testing room until the appropriate time to leave.

While much of this chapter outlines ideals and best-case scenarios, minimizing distractions within the testing space and broader practice environment supports valid testing. Conversations around the sensory experience of clients assist psychometrists in understanding the role they play in obtaining valid data, outside of standardized test administration.

11 Redirecting and Responding to Clients During Testing

Clients arrive at our offices with diverse expectations and emotions. I will never forget the teenager who, after completing the first subtest in one of our sessions, blurted out his immense feelings of relief that *this* was what he'd be doing all day. He shared that he thought he would be "hooked up to a whole bunch of monitors and forced to sit in a dark room for hours." We had a good laugh, and I felt like I could visibly see his anxiety subsiding. He was pleasantly surprised by the actual testing process and remained a very eager participant thereafter.

Despite our best efforts to share information about what the day will entail, it seems that the majority of clients we see are not entirely sure of what to expect when they arrive for the testing appointment. We likely shared an overview of the day with the parent or family member scheduling the appointment, but this information is not always passed to the client actually engaging in our testing process. Thus, those initial moments upon arriving to the office can be the most critical in terms of setting expectations and, more importantly, putting the client at ease. I tell my psychometrist to assume that the client knows absolutely nothing about the day and to take the time after initially greeting him or her to set the facts straight.

Upon Arrival to the Office

Depending on the setting in which you work, it is possible that you have a dedicated front-office person to greet patients upon arrival. In other cases, particularly in private practices, the psychometrist may also act as the front-office staff, and thus your psychometrist may be the one to greet patients when they arrive. Regardless of who is the first to welcome the client, it can be immensely helpful to review key points to convey to clients upon arrival, as well as ways to modify one's welcoming remarks based on age. Here are a few sample scripts that I review with my psychometrist, although it can be helpful to tailor the welcoming remarks to your particular setting and population.

YOUNG CHILD: "Hello, my name is Jane Smith and we are going to be doing a lot of fun activities together today. This doctor's office is a little bit

DOI: 10.4324/9781003098010-12

different, because we won't look in your ears, we won't listen to your heart, and there are absolutely no shots! We will be doing things like drawing pictures, solving puzzles, and playing games on a computer or iPad. You aren't going to earn a grade for these activities, and you are not expected to get every answer right. All I ask is that you try your very best! We can take breaks to check in on mom/dad/caregiver, or to use the bathroom. We will do most things this morning, take a nice break for lunch, and finish up this afternoon. Do you have any questions? Are you ready to see the toys in my activity room?"

SCHOOL AGE: "Hello, my name is Jane Smith and we will be working together today. We will be completing activities together today like solving puzzles, playing computer games, or seeing how much information you can remember. Sometimes the activities may be similar to things you do in school, while others may be a little different. You can let me know if you need a break, and as long as we aren't right in the middle of an activity, we can likely take that break. We do these activities with kids of all ages, so some things may feel super easy—other things may be more challenging. All I ask is that you try your best! Do you have any questions? Are you ready to get started?"

TEENAGER: "Hello, my name is Jane Smith and we will be working together today. We are going to complete activities like defining words, solving puzzles, and seeing how much information you can remember. While you can't pass or fail these tests, it is very important that you try your best. We give these tests to people of all ages, so you are not expected to get everything right or to know all of the answers. If you totally hate something we are doing, bear with me for about 10 or 15 minutes, and we will likely move on to the next task. Do you have any questions? Are you ready to get started?"

ADULT/GERIATRIC: "Hello, my name is Jane Smith and I will be working with you today. We will be doing a variety of tests—some that will be quite easy for you and others that are meant to be challenging. You are not expected to know all the answers or get everything right. All I ask is that you try your best on everything that we do. If you are getting tired or frustrated, let me know and we can take a break as soon as that task is over. Also, nothing we do here is a secret, so if you have a question about why we are doing a particular task, I would be glad to tell you about it, so feel free to ask."

A word of caution: while scripts and planned remarks are all well and good, reading the room can also be incredibly beneficial. I know of one psychometrist who walked into a waiting room to greet the client for the day, and after quickly sharing her name and title, she launched into a whole comprehensive summary about what all the client would be doing, how many hours they'd be working together, and so on. Well, it turned out that the client was somewhat unwillingly dragged to the appointment by a loving family member, and this set the client off on a long and emotionally charged rant about why she didn't need testing, how her memory was just fine, how forcing her to do testing against her will was not right—*especially* given all the hours it was expected to take—not an ideal way to start building rapport.

Needless to say, that psychometrist learned a lesson that day: starting with a few minutes of rapport-building before launching into your own agenda can allow for meaningful data gathering and make your life a whole lot easier. Getting a sense of the client's general mood or feelings about testing can be gleaned in the first moments of the getting-to-know you chat. I encourage psychometrists to ask the client "so what do you know about what we will be doing today?" or "what is your understanding about what we will be doing today?" as a way to explore the space for those clients who don't provide a lot of initial intel.

Once Settled in the Testing Room

Setting up the testing space prior to your client's arrival is key (see previous chapter for details). However, once the psychometrist and client are seated and comfortable, it is perfectly reasonable, and often encouraged, that the psychometrist check in with the client briefly again. I encourage my psychometrist to say something like:

> Alright, so this is where we will be for a good bit of today. Feel free to leave your water bottle nearby, but I'd like to ask you to switch off your phone and put it away until breaks. Now that you've had a few minutes to think about the information we discussed in the lobby, do you have any questions about what we will do today, or are you ready to jump in?

Some clients will say they are just ready to get this over with, and testing begins without issue. Others may admit to being distracted or anxious in the waiting room, at which point the psychometrist may re-review expectations. For those psychometrists who notice the client is easily distracted or perhaps a bit emotional in the waiting room, it can be a great time to say something along the lines of "well, I know I shared a whole lot of information with you in the waiting room, but to briefly review." Attempting to normalize a client's inability to recall details of what was shared in the initial waiting room chat (whether caused by distraction, anxiety, or otherwise) will further put the client at ease.

With pediatric clients, I encourage my psychometrist to take the initial few minutes to ask about hobbies, friends, favorite television shows, or something that conveys interest in getting to know them. This can be an informal method of language sampling or a way to get a sense of their social communication. After our one- to two-minute conversation is finished, the psychometrist can present some sort of preview of the structure going forward. For example:

> It is so cool that we both like hiking! I can't wait to hear more about the different trails you've been on! So, part of my job today is to get us through lots of different activities. When we are doing the activities, I am going to work very hard to keep us focused, but during breaks or lunch, you can tell me more about your adventures!

With very young clients, it can be helpful to pull out a white piece of paper and draw boxes to set the plan for the morning: "we are going to do 3 activities, and then we can take a break for snack." With this pre-testing stage set, the psychometrist can then easily redirect the client "remember—I am task manager so tell me that story at break" or "first this, then break." If all else fails, tangible reinforcers can be added to the mix when assessing pediatric clients. I share a plethora of stickers with my psychometrist, so sometimes younger clients earn stickers for each subtest they complete. Other times, parents may choose to use the opportunity to go out to lunch instead of eating their packed-from-home lunch as a method to increase motivation. In some instances, a prize chest or prize closet can be dangled, but as we all know, the prize is only earned with compliance, and if the child complies, the prize must be awarded.

It can be helpful to chat with parents before the child's arrival about things that may be motivating to the child and share this with your psychometrist ahead of time. While putting a reinforcement plan together on the fly certainly works, any advanced warning can support smooth transitions through the testing. Similarly, if a child's worst nightmare is math, starting with math subtests is sure to reduce compliant engagement thereafter, so providing your psychometrist with some context around known areas of difficulty can help support their planning process.

Nonverbal Communication: Unintended Negative Impacts on Rapport-Building

During the training stages, I talk openly with my psychometrist about how their behavior can directly or indirectly impact the client. For example, if you forget your stopwatch, it may be tempting to use your phone's timer instead. However, the teenager across from you might suspect that you are using your phone for other purposes (texting, etc.), which can foster distrust and interfere with the testing. If a phone must be used, I instruct the psychometrist to explain to the client why it is being used and place it on airplane mode (thus no calls, texts, or otherwise can come through).

Another critical point in discussing our behavior as test administrators is the way we take notes. I recall a young, bright boy who quickly picked up on my notation strategies for one particular assessment. In an attempt at increasing efficiency, I would only circle those answers he got incorrect. In my mind, this was a way to keep testing moving forward and I would easily know those that were not circled were answered correctly. Towards the end of the assessment, he said, "well, I must have gotten that wrong because you marked your paper." I quickly shifted gears and made sure to note all responses in the same manner; correct or incorrect. Another time this may arise is during a verbal digit-span task, as the examiner may only write down the incorrect response following on a longer string of numbers. While many clients may be oblivious to these subtleties, those who are more attuned to nonverbal communication may be quick to interpret your behavior.

Verbal Praise at Any Age: Beyond Tangible Reinforcers

Just as what we write can be telling, our verbal responses can also lead clients to draw conclusions about their performance. Particularly with newer or slightly more anxious psychometrists, I notice a near impulsive "good" or "that's right" when testing. We want the client to feel encouraged, and so often there is this natural inclination to respond positively to answers provided. While it can be hard to train oneself to remain silent after each response, some sort of appropriately placed feedback can be helpful. For example, following a particularly challenging task, it is perfectly reasonable to say something like "those got tricky, so nice job sticking with me through the end" or "I can tell you are really working hard on these tasks—keep up the hard work!"

Particularly when nervous ourselves, such as in the case of an early-in-training psychometrist, we may have more of a tendency to provide validation or positive encouragement in testing. If the psychometrist accidentally says some sort of confirmatory feedback early in a subtest (e.g., "good," "yes," "correct," after any of the early questions), I let them know that the burden is on them then to say "good" after every single one, regardless of whether the client gets it right or wrong. After a few occasions of repeating "good" over and over, the reflexive positive reinforcement stops.

So, what is the best way to support our clients or verbally encourage ongoing engagement? In pediatric populations, labeled verbal praise such as "I like the way you are sitting so calmly in your chair" or "look at how hard you are working, I love to see you trying your best" can keep the child eager to seek your praise. With teens and young adults, I find less is more, and the occasional statement like "that was a really tricky one but I can tell you were working hard" will suffice. In older adults, it can be perfectly appropriate to acknowledge that perhaps they have not engaged in these types of activities in quite some time. Normalizing this experience while continuing to praise good effort can both reduce anxieties and validate potential frustrations.

The Psychometrist's Role in the Testing Experience

It is hard to adequately convey the importance of the psychometrists' role in the testing process. Beyond standardized administration, the behavior our psychometrists bring to the testing room has a direct impact on clients.

It is often the psychometrist who will decide on the order of administration of tests. While I tend to have a more collaborative discussion with early-in-training psychometrists, more seasoned psychometrists will take my test list and create their own plan for execution. It is therefore quite important to help the psychometrist understand ahead of time if the client has conveyed clear areas of difficulty. If the client coming in has difficulty with memory or math computation, it is best to steer clear of those tasks to start. That said, consideration of fatigue, testing priorities, and the possibility that the client may not complete all testing on the battery makes strategic planning on the part of the psychometrist critically important. Painting with a broad brush, I think of the testing day as a normal curve: begin with a task that is relatively easy and straightforward, progress to more complex tasks throughout the morning and early afternoon, then end again with easier or straightforward tasks. Also adding to this mix, the "most critical" tests should be prioritized, while "it would be great to have" testing pushed later in the day.

This is also a good time to help the psychometrist understand their role in the client experience. Often, the clients are coming in either nervous or unaware of what to expect in the day's evaluation. By conveying confidence, coming across as calm yet knowledgeable and supportive, we can allay some client anxieties from the start. As testing progresses, monitoring the client's fatigue, keeping the client on task and progressing satisfactorily, and providing appropriate praise for effort can maintain a positive experience for all.

Collateral Informants and/or Parents in the Testing Room

With very few exceptions, there should be no additional people in the room with a psychometrist and client during testing. When I complete testing with infants, I have parents in the room to discuss whether they have seen certain behaviors at home or to maintain comfort of the infant. In young children, particularly preschool age or younger, parents may be asked to join their child on the walk to the testing in the room or to assist the child with getting settled in a new environment (the testing space). Having cooperative toys available in the testing room as a way of transitioning from waiting room to testing room can comfort the child and immediately help them to engage in something enjoyable. I will join in a cooperative play or a game with parent and child to start and then give the parent a discrete indication that they are free to move back to the waiting space. At times, particularly with infants or extremely young children, a parent may be of benefit for the initial moments of the transition, but then I will ask them to unobtrusively head back to the waiting room once the child is engaged in the first testing tasks. I will also be quick to transition to new tests so as to keep the attention of the child from wandering to, "hey, where is my mom?" This is an excellent example as to why it is important to be prepared before clients arrive for testing, particularly our youngest of clients.

Given the many position papers from national and international neuropsychological societies, I won't go into the rationale behind why third-party observers should not be permitted in the testing room (*see National Academy of Neuropsychology, 1999*). I do, however, empower my psychometrist to stand firm if there is a request to observe, but also to alert me immediately if the issue remains unresolved prior to taking the client back to the testing room.

Sample Clients and Considerations for Responding

One of my favorite parts of reviewing the psychometrist surveys that I collected for this project was reading about folks' "most memorable" clients. Themes arose around the difficulties that we face with certain types of clients, and while I fully acknowledge that all clients are unique and bring with them their own experiences and circumstances, the following sections review broad behaviors and methods to manage those behaviors within the testing context.

Ants in My Pants: The Hyperactive Client

I immediately think of school-aged children when I think about my most hyperactive clients, and this seems to be a trend among survey respondents. For children who cannot sit still, the following behavioral strategies are suggested:

- Plan "wiggle breaks" frequently between activities (every one to two tasks or subtests) and join the child in jumping jacks, high-knee marching in place, or Simon Says.
- Allow the child to stand during verbal tasks or those that do not require them to look at materials or manipulate objects.
- Be sure the child is seated in a non-wheeled chair and scoot the chair close to the table. If there are chairs with arms, they can be helpful in setting the boundaries for wiggles and maintaining the child in the chair.
- While we have all had that client who picks up and plays with anything and everything on the table, intentionally providing a fidget toy, stress ball, or other object to allow the child a specific method for expending energy can help them to maintain focus on the task at hand. Note when these supports are in place and to attempt testing without them initially.

As we know, these data in understanding the differences in performance with and without the fidget toy can be beneficial to schools and other providers working with the child in the future.
- Informally "hypothesis test," when appropriate, with clients. For example, if the child is kicking the table underneath them, politely ask that they keep their feet still. Note whether or not this behavior reemerges and whether it appears to be unintentional.

This, No Wait, That, No Wait, Actually This One: The Impulsive Client

Though sometimes hard to do, it is best to stay one step ahead of the impulsive client. When administering tasks, I often try the following:

- When appropriate, remind the client that there is no time limit for the task, and thus it is appropriate to encourage them to review all answers before verbalizing their response.
- Clear all unnecessary items from the table in order to reduce the likelihood that manipulatives will be impulsively grabbed, moved, or tinkered with.
- Preemptively tell the client that it is my job to do things like turn pages and decide when tasks are complete.
- There may be times when it is perfectly appropriate to tell clients to sit on their hands if they are incapable of inhibiting motor responses. This is obviously more difficult when verbal responses are an option.
- It also may be beneficial to slow the pace of administration, ever so slightly, in order to visibly demonstrate what you hope to see from the client. In these "teachable moments," see if the client responds by mirroring your own behavior—again, providing rich behavioral data to supplement recommendations for support.

Are You Married? The Disinhibited Client

Working with neurologically compromised individuals, it is likely that most psychometrists will come across a disinhibited client in their professional journey. While I cannot possibly list the many inappropriate or intrusive comments that have been made by our disinhibited clients, here are a few tips and tricks on how best to respond:

- In response to any question about your family, personal life, or otherwise, politely tell the client we are here for them and that you don't answer questions about your personal life in these sessions. A respectfully firm yet direct approach is best.
- Unfortunately, if these comments are not addressed immediately, some clients will see how far they can push boundaries. It may start with

something seemingly benign—like "where are you from?"—but it is important to set clear boundaries from the onset of personal questions—remember, if you give an inch, the disinhibited client just may take the mile.

- If the client engages in any kind of inappropriate self-touching, ask the client to keep his or her hands on the table during tasks.
- Like the impulsive client, be mindful of the items on the desk or testing space and keep all unnecessary books, notes, pens, and supplies off the table.

Why I Ought to . . .: The Aggressive Client

Thankfully, in my professional career, I've had very few direct experiences with aggressive clients, although many colleagues shared stories for this book. Based on others' experiences, the following suggestions are made:

- For a particularly aggressive child, it can be helpful to sit them in a corner or position the table so that they are unable to quickly dash to the door, move about, or hurt themselves. This strategic positioning of the table restricts their movement as a method of keeping them safe.
- Much of the advice shared about aggressive clients was to remove oneself from the situation as quickly as possible and to keep everyone safe. Therefore, being sure the psychometrist's chair is closest to the door to facilitate rapid exit, if needed, is essential. When an aggressive client feels the need to act out, the goal is to remove others from the situation, allow for a period of calming, and to reengage when folks are ready.
- For those clients where the frustration is visible early on (clenched fists, loud sighing, etc.), provide a stress ball or more frequent breaks to ease frustration.

Am I Doing This Right? The Anxious Client

Many clients arrive to our offices with anxiety, even those without a formal anxiety disorder diagnosis. It can be unnerving to enter a situation where your weaknesses are "laid out in front of you," or where you may have an opportunity to learn that your thinking skills are no longer as sharp as they used to be. While some level of anxiety can be adaptive, it is best to put the client's mind at ease, as much as possible, before the formal testing begins. For example:

- Acknowledge the client's anxiety and normalize those feelings as much as possible.
- Reassure the client that while some things may be tricky or frustrating, others they may find quite enjoyable.

- As testing progresses, provide positive reinforcement of effort and acknowledge the client's willingness to stick with tasks that become challenging or frustrating.
- Strike a balance with feedback; too much positive reinforcement, and the client may think you are not being genuine. Further, it can be tiring to both psychometrist and client over time!

I Just Don't See the Point of Any of This: The Argumentative or Defiant Client

Sometimes, no matter how hard we or our client's families try, the client is just simply not interested and frustrated to be at the testing session. To the extent that you are still able to gather valid data, the following tips can assist with keeping progress moving forward:

- Planned ignoring can be the best way to reduce the unwanted behavior we see in the testing room. While it is impolite to blatantly ignore questions or genuine engagement, it is perfectly acceptable to not acknowledge complaints, minor grievances, or other relatively benign comments made by the client. For example, once a client said "dumb," "ridiculous," "silly," or some other adjective after each question on a visual puzzle task. Despite these comments, she was getting the correct answers, so I continued with the testing and allowed her to express her thoughts without response from me.
- At times, particularly with clients who come to the session with memory concerns, it may be appropriate to review the likelihood of frustration or expectation that he or she will not get every answer correct. If arguments are stemming from frustration, increasing breaks can help.
- Finally, it is good to remind the client that they are not being held against his or her will and that they are able to leave at any time. With this in mind, it is appropriate to follow up with the family to assist in reinforcing the reasons the client was referred in the first place, in hopes that testing can continue as scheduled.

This Is Hard and I Am Terrible at Everything: The Sad Client

Depression is a common comorbidity with neurological illness or injury; thus, these clients are often seated in our offices. While it is not our job to cheer them up or brighten their day, maintaining a positive affect and aligning with the client can establish rapport and assist with the timely completion of tasks. Specifically:

- Start with a particularly easy task that has a high likelihood of success.
- Praise the client for effort and engagement.

- Offer breaks, as needed, but also maintain an upbeat and forward-moving pace so as to keep the client engaged.
- It can be worthwhile to chat with the client about some of their interests or hobbies, in order to have things to "cheer them on" in the later portions of testing. For example, I was able to remind a client of how proud his granddaughter would be to hear of his hard work, and that pepped him up for the later afternoon testing tasks. Having some sort of personal connection can be a powerful motivator!

That Reminds Me of This One Time . . . : The Chatty Client

Sometimes, we are the only appointment on our client's schedule for the entire week. This is their "big day out" and you are the main source of social engagement. Thus, the client may want to share many stories, learn about your life, and treat this session like a coffee chat. It can be helpful to set clear boundaries from the start, such as:

- "Hello, client. It is my job to keep us on track. I don't mean to be rude, but sometimes I will tell you that we can't swap stories and we need to keep moving through the testing tasks. I may say things like, "I want to hear your stories but we have a lot more to do, let's get through these next X number of tasks and then we can take a break to chat."
- It can be helpful to then refer to this prior statement, "remember, I am in charge of keeping us on task!" in order to thwart the next story to be shared.

Pediatric Clients: Broad Considerations

While many pediatric strategies have already been reviewed earlier, here are a few additional suggestions for the pediatric setting:

- For young children, toys or some sort of cooperative play items can help ease the child into the testing space and allow the parent to slip back to the waiting room.
- Ample preparation by the psychometrist ahead of time will keep testing moving forward and keep clients on track.
- Organize supplies so they are easily accessible and there is minimal downtime between tests.
- Use a visual schedule or sticker chart to provide concrete benchmarks for breaks. Setting clear structure assists the child with understanding what comes next.
- Providing a small toy or prize box at the end-of-session can be a successful method of maintaining engagement if sticker charts lose their luster.

Reference

National Academy of Neuropsychology. (1999). Presence of third-party observers during neuropsychological testing. *Archives of Clinical Neuropsychology, 15*(5), 379–380.

12 Behavioral Observations

Crucial Observations to Support Diagnostic Accuracy

Humans are naturally observant beings. We watch our partners engage in a daily breakfast routine, see the neighbors' puppy playing outdoors, or glance toward a child having a meltdown in the grocery store. Observing the behavior of those in our environment is ongoing. So how do we as neuropsychologists break down the components of behavior that we are most interested in capturing during an assessment? When training my psychometrists, I often joke that I do not need a "play-by-play" of exactly what the client is doing (e.g., client tucked hair behind ear) or potential hypotheses (e.g., client sniffled-possible cold?) for each behavior. I also explain that there are behaviors I am particularly attuned to during each type of test (more on this later). However, in general, behaviors begin simply and become more complex. In the sections that follow, I review the hierarchy of behavioral observation within each broad domain of functioning as one potential framework for training.

Setting matters when considering the types of behaviors that might be observed or might need to be addressed. When I worked on an inpatient unit, observations of behavior included changes in arousal or span of time experiencing confusion or agitation. Although the time spent with the client was briefer, the observations were equally as important for updating treatment goals and serially monitoring change over time. Therefore, the observations you are hoping to glean from your psychometrist can and likely will be somewhat tailored to your setting and the types of patients you work with each day.

In addition, there are certain settings that may require additional training in appropriate responses to medical emergencies. For example, a psychometrist on an epilepsy monitoring unit requires more in-depth training on seizure protocols than a psychometrist in a private practice setting. While keeping context in mind, the following is a brief synopsis of how to structure behavioral observation gathering with your psychometrist. As mentioned subsequently, newer psychometrists may benefit from a structured form (see Behavioral Observation handout in the Appendix) or checklist, which can be tailored to a particular setting or age demographic.

DOI: 10.4324/9781003098010-13

Behavioral Observations

Those early evaluations where I am administering all assessments and my psychometry trainee is observing provide an opportunity to really delve into the observational process. A lot of this learning occurs through direct observation of the neuropsychologist; however, not everything can be covered during the initial training phases. Sometimes, what may seem like an obviously notable behavior to one person may seem completely typical and inconsequential to another. Hence, behavioral observation is a key component of training that is worth spending time on. I also encourage my psychometrists to review Kaplan's article on the process approach, as it can provide further insight into the rationale behind *how* a client arrived at a score, not just the score itself (Kaplan, 1988). While there are many chapters and texts on behavioral observation, it is up to you and your typical style in terms of structuring this aspect of training. Next, I review some of the areas that I touch upon in the initial training of my psychometrist.

General Appearance

First, I like to document some basic information about my initial impressions of the client. Did the individual arrive to the appointment on time, were they late, and were they aware? Did they come alone, or accompanied by a partner? What was their general state upon arrival? How was their grooming and hygiene? Did they appear properly dressed for the occasion? How is their physical stature, and do they appear their stated age? Are they assisted by any visible devices such as wheelchair, cane, hearing aids, or glasses?

Having the psychometrist make basic notes about the client's general appearance allows the neuropsychologist the opportunity to decipher any meaning when later reviewing the client's full file. When talking about the general appearance of clients, I emphasize to my psychometrist that this is not a judgment of a client's style or a comment on a client's fashion sense. This is one opportunity to get a sense of whether the individual is regularly able to complete activities of daily living (showering, hair combing, teeth brushing), if they are able to choose an outfit that is sensible for the weather and appropriately comfortable or reflective of their understanding that they will be at a doctor's appointment for a few hours. As the neuropsychologist, I can then consider whether clothes that are oversized or tightly fitting reflect concerning changes to one's dietary regimen, or whether an elderly client might be forgetting to eat meals.

Arousal and Attention

While we administer various formal measures of attention, I ask my psychometrist to note key behaviors. For example, was the client falling asleep or nodding off during tasks? Was the client able to sustain basic attention for brief tasks, or were they easily distracted? Did the client appear hyper-attuned to the air conditioning clicking on, the conversation of a passerby in the hallway, or a car alarm ringing outside? Was redirection back to the task helpful? Tallying the number of breaks required or the length of time between breaks provided can also shed light on the client's need to get up and move about or difficulties sticking with the examiner.

Executive Processes

Executive processes include responsivity, initiation, speed of processing, working memory, flexibility, impulsivity, planning, organization, self-regulation and self-monitoring. First, is the client responsive to your bids for engagement? Correctness, appropriateness, or relevancy of the response is irrelevant at this point; it is simply to gauge whether any kind of response occurs. Second, does the client spontaneously initiate any kind of behavior (e.g., asking questions, sharing information, passing materials, grabbing at materials presented, getting up from the chair, removing a sweater or outerwear), considering both verbal and nonverbal methods and the age appropriateness of the initiated act. How is the client's pace of responding—slow, immediate, rushed? Are they able to keep information in mind, like task directions for example, or do you find it necessary to repeat or clarify task demands? How does the client respond to transitions between tests or the display of new materials? Are they rigid or inflexible, or can they transition easily? Do they get stuck on activities? Comment on the level of distractibility movement outside of the chair, general activity level, and whether they impulsively reach for items. In contrast, are they apathetic, lethargic, or slumped over in the chair? How was their approach to problem-solving? Did they make a plan, or jump right in? Did they respond to feedback? Was there evidence that the client was able to self-monitor their own behavior, or did they appear to have insight into their areas of difficulty?

Speech and Language

Often speech and language are grouped together, but it can be helpful to discuss each separately when training a psychometrist. First, it is important to comment upon hearing: was the client's hearing adequate for the evaluation, or did they require assistive devices to hear the psychometrist? I then discuss quality and quantity of both speech and language. Regarding speech, I touch upon the client's articulation or fluency; is there any stammering or stuttering? How is the client's vocal quality, perhaps raspy, monotone, or airy, and how is the rhythm or volume of their speech? Are there notable articulation errors? I then move on to language, touching upon word retrieval, vocabulary use, and grammar, as well as note any irrelevant phrases, confabulatory statements, and the quality or appropriateness of verbal utterances. Comments on echolalia (repeating other's words), palilalia (repeating their own words), or language errors would be noted in this section. With regard to receptive language, comments around comprehension of instructions or needs for repetition, appropriateness of responses, or requests for clarification would be noted. It can be helpful to discuss any contrasts between formal language measures and informal conversational language. When there are concerns about speech or language, I ask the psychometrist to make note of specific examples in order to tailor recommendations.

Social Pragmatics

Social pragmatics can be assessed formally or informally, but observations are geared toward appropriateness of eye contact, response to nonverbal cues, gestures or redirection, reciprocity in social engagement (e.g., turn taking), flexibility or rigidity in topic maintenance, and general comfort in the exchange. If the psychometrist feels that they are working hard to sustain an interaction or feel trapped in a conversation despite social signals indicating a desire to transition from the topic at hand, reflection upon their own personal response to engaging with the client can assist them with making notes around social pragmatics. For example, if they feel like they are working hard to sustain conversation, just imagine how the client's same-aged peers experience them. I may also touch further upon aspects of speech (e.g., monotone, inappropriate volume, mechanical) in this discussion.

Visuoperception

As with other areas described earlier, visuoperception begins at a basic level and progresses to more complex tasks. These abilities first depend on the client's visual acuity, which some neuropsychologists prefer to measure prior to initiating the evaluation. Once that is deemed adequate, I first discuss any concerns with basic visual scanning (e.g., was there concern for neglect? Did the client only look at one section of the page?), and the client's ability to attend to his or her environment. How successful was the client when walking to the assessment room? Did they navigate the space appropriately, or did they bump into objects or misjudge spacing? How did the client respond to basic visual discrimination or matching tasks? Did they get tripped up on small details? When a stimulus book or other materials were placed in front of the client, did they move it toward their face, or perhaps turn their head to view the item? How did the client respond when drawing or copying (visuomotor integration)? Informally, I may ask the client about navigating their home environment—any falls, misperceptions, occasions where the individual meant to place a glass on the table but it landed on the floor?

Learning and Memory

When administering learning and memory tasks, many notes may arise. In the verbal domain, how does the individual respond to contextual (e.g., story) versus noncontextual (e.g., list) information? Did they appear overwhelmed? How did they respond to repetition? Did it seem to help or stress them out more? When providing cues or multiple-choice options, did the client recall more information, or did it appear to confuse them? This information allows me to get a sense of strategies that may benefit the client. In the visual domain, I ask my psychometrist to comment on the approach to drawing (if it is an aspect of the test) or the method the client uses to identify aspects of the visual information presented (e.g., he recalled information in the top row, but struggled more with later rows; with repetition, he always got the first two shapes, but then could not recall the later designs.)

Motor

Motor observations include both gross and fine motor abilities. Though I have likely seen the client in the waiting room, I ask the psychometrist to comment on the client's transition to the testing room—whether they require assistance or walk with any notable gait or balance difficulties. I ask that the psychometrist note any prosthetics or other devices to assist with movement, leg, or arm braces. During testing, if I have not already asked, I ask the psychometrist to note the client's upper extremity preference, pencil grip position, and whether they anchor the paper when writing. When administering tasks with manipulatives, was the client observed to use both hands? When writing, was there uniformity in the margin size, letter formation, straightness or accuracy of word placement on a line, and how was the client's pencil pressure (e.g., if the psychometrist had to repeatedly sharpen or switch out a dull pencil during the testing)?

Mood/Affect

Mood and affect are often the first things that psychometrists note in training. It is very easy to spot an agitated client or a flat, apathetic one. I like to note concerns for mood lability, poor frustration tolerance, or any changes to mood across the day (e.g., very excited to be here in the morning, but complaining about length of testing by the end). I continue to ask for behaviors (not diagnoses) such as sighing, tearfulness, excessive laughter, or giggling when task difficulty increased. I also talk about common anxiety behaviors, such as biting of lip, chewing on nails or other objects (e.g., pencils), or fidgeting with paperclips. I also want to understand the appropriateness of the client's mood or affect. Did they smile or laugh appropriately? Did they discuss sad events while grinning ear to ear, or look sad while discussing a recent joyful event? How was the client's overall attitude toward testing?

Sensory

Sensory sensitivities can be harder to pick up on but are important to note if they arise in testing. For example, for visual sensitivities, how does the client respond to changes in light or the repositioning of objects on the table? Are they wearing glasses? Do they prefer to view things a particular way or tilt their head when looking at stimuli? Regarding auditory sensitivities, how does the client respond to sudden noises, even subtle noises such as the air conditioning clicking on or a passerby in the hallway? Does the individual request repetition of information, speak loudly, or request the psychometrist to speak louder, move closer, or farther away from the table? How does the client respond to touch or something touching him or her, such as the offering of a high five or the feeling of the pegs for the pegboard, for example? While many times these sensitivities are shared during the intake interview, these behaviors when they arise are important to note.

Judgment of Safety and Effort

Finally, I want the psychometrist to be keenly aware of concerns for neglect or abuse. I review the importance of notifying me immediately if the client makes comments that suggest neglect or abuse, or if they verbalize any statements around suicidal/homicidal thoughts, intent, or plan. I finally want to get a sense from the psychometrist if they feel the client was giving optimal effort or trying his or her best throughout the evaluation. While embedded and free-standing measures will support a valid profile, it can provide insight into how a teacher or spouse may experience the client on a day-to-day basis (e.g., "he is lazy" or "she doesn't care").

Behaviors, Not Diagnoses

One of the biggest comments on survey results from neuropsychologists revealed desires for psychometrists to discuss observed behaviors, not diagnostic impressions. For example, instead of saying the child was anxious, neuropsychologists find it more helpful for the psychometrist to discuss specific examples, such as the child said her stomach hurt when working on the reading task or the child had a concerned look on her face when presented with a verbal list learning task. Providing specific examples of atypical or unique behaviors (e.g., "she chewed her shirt sleeve every time I brought up the math task") can then assist the neuropsychologist with determining the appropriate diagnosis.

Test-Specific Behavioral Observations

What can be initially uncomfortable for a neuropsychologist who is newly implementing psychometrist testing support is not being in the room as the child is completing testing tasks. "How will they know what I am looking for, and what if they miss something?" During initial training, I find that sitting down with my psychometrist and talking through the pertinent behavioral observations I am making for each test can be particularly helpful in directing their observations. I also review with my psychometrist the observations I made for each test when they observed my administration of testing (e.g., Ashendorf et al., 2013). In this way, I am able to tie in specific examples ("did you see how Johnny. . .).

"Normal" Behaviors

There are a few additional points worth considering when training your psychometrist in behavioral observations. First, it may be beneficial to review developmental stages for common behaviors, particularly if you are working in a pediatric-heavy or pediatric-only practice. For example, it is perfectly appropriate for a four-year-old to reverse letters, but this behavior is not typically seen in a nine-year-old. While there is no substitute for a course in child development, it can at least be beneficial to review major milestones and expectations around certain common behaviors.

Focusing on the Negative

Something that can be challenging is our tendency to focus on the "bad" or atypical behaviors observed during the evaluation. "Susie was always out of her chair and when she was seated she repeatedly kicked my leg." While it may be easy to note the negatives, equally as important is to be able to consistently spot the positives. One of my favorite parts of working with a psychometrist is the post-evaluation debriefing session. Often, I want to know about particular behaviors of concern. However, I intentionally make time for a discussion of the strengths observed during testing. For example:

> Despite Susie's hyperactivity and poor self-regulation, she also repeated to herself "Come on, Susie, you can do this!" when working on new or unfamiliar tasks. She loved zoo stickers and worked very hard when reminded of her sticker chart. When I asked her to stop kicking my leg she complied, so it really wasn't personal—she simply couldn't help it!

Notes on Your Own Behavior

While this chapter is predominantly about the observations we make about our clients, it is also a time to consider those behaviors that the client may or may not be observing in you. Specifically, it is important to be aware of our own behavior, and how our behavior during testing may impact the client. For example, let's pretend for a moment that you are flipping through the early pages of a visual task and the client is repeatedly answering correctly. You are able to quickly flip through, until the client makes an inevitable error. You pause, write down the incorrect response, and then return to flipping. Right there, you have subtly indicated to your client that something changed, and perhaps those who are keenly aware of your responses to them (e.g., anxious clients) now feel they did something wrong. Test takers are often more aware of your testing cadence than you'd expect, and thus it is important to be discrete and intentional with the markings we make on test protocols. I review with my psychometrists the practice of making uniform markings (e.g., writing down all digits during digit span, even when they are all correct) so as not to lead the client into thinking they did something incorrectly. If they do need to take a quick pause or make a note, I encourage them to wait until the end of the subtest or jot the note while the client is looking at the next question.

Along the same lines, often we need to time our clients completing certain tasks. While some find the old-school stopwatches cumbersome, I find they are particularly important with teenage clients who can become unduly distracted by a phone timer. In a pinch, it is best to be open with your client about your phone if you must use it. It is better to say something like "I have my phone here today to time some of your responses during testing. I have placed it on airplane mode and will only be using it to time, as needed." We are modeling the behaviors we want to see in our clients, so it is highly hypocritical to tell a client to put away their phone, only to pop yours out moments later. Practice what you preach, and purchase that stopwatch pronto!

Finally, I discuss with the psychometrist the importance of noting the sequence of testing and key behaviors noted during particular tasks. In this way, the psychometrist may note patterns (e.g., "math appeared very taxing and client tanked on verbal list learning task thereafter"). Noting the sequence of testing and behaviors that are consistent with it allows for detailed, sequential notes about the quality of responses or emotional reactions our tasks elicit.

Testing the Limits

The final section in behavioral observations is a discussion around testing of limits. While I encourage all psychometrists to stick to the book and discontinue as dictated by the manual early on in training, more seasoned psychometrists should be taught to test the limits in certain circumstances. For example, if the client is close to completing a block design task but is outside of the time limit, I often allow the client to finish in order to build rapport and to reduce the possibility of frustration at being prematurely stopped when the client is "so close." If the client answers multiple questions correctly but is outside of the time limit for each of them, I may encourage the psychometrist to continue to get a sense of how the client would have performed if time was not a factor. In most cases, I ask the psychometrist to touch base with me prior to limit testing unless it is on a test we've previously discussed.

While deviation from standardized instructions is not discussed until later in training, I do encourage my psychometrist to be a detective with the client whenever possible. For example, if a client comes in speaking rapidly, what happens if the psychometrist speaks slowly and quietly? Does the client mirror the psychometrist? Is there a change in the interaction? Another example, suppose a child is tapping a pencil on the desk, how do they respond to a verbal request to put the pencil down? Do they reengage in the behavior shortly thereafter? What if the pencil is moved farther from the client (but still within reach)? All of this is rich qualitative data and can help me later when tailoring my recommendations for home, school/vocational, and community-based supports.

When to Call in Backup, and When to Press Forward

There are a few instances when the psychometrist should immediately call for the neuropsychologist. As discussed earlier, any verbalizations around suicide, homicide, neglect, abuse, or other illegal behaviors should be brought immediately to the attention of the supervising neuropsychologist. Even behaviors such as excessive tearfulness warrant a conversation between the psychometrist and the neuropsychologist before the client leaves. Further, if a client has a seizure or medical emergency, calling for help and alerting the neuropsychologist immediately are key. In fact, training around possible medical emergencies and particular protocols (e.g., seizure response in an epilepsy clinic) should be rehearsed so that a psychometrist feels well prepared in case of an emergency.

There are also instances when, despite the client's preferences, it may be best to press forward with the evaluation. A child who is whining that they don't want to be at the evaluation should finish at least a few tasks before "earning" a break to see a parent. Similarly, older adults who state that they were forced to attend the evaluation should be encouraged to complete some of the testing before returning to the waiting room to see a loved one. While we do not hold clients hostage and they are free to leave at any time, there is a clear reason they were referred to our service, and we want to do our best to get as much testing done or as much information obtained before the client leaves for the day.

I included my most recent Behavioral Observation form in the Appendix, but I know that many forms have been shared on professional listservs and among colleagues. It also may be your preference to engage in an open conversation with the psychometrist following each patient and not rely upon a standardized form at all. Whether checklist, open-ended response form, or in-depth conversation, training for a psychometrist in noting key behavioral observations is essential.

References

Ashendorf, L., Swenson, R., & Libon, D.J. (Eds.). (2013). *The Boston Process Approach to Neuropsychological Assessment: A Practitioner's Guide*. New York, NY: Oxford University Press.

Kaplan, E. (1988). A process approach to neuropsychological assessment. In M. Dennis, E. Kaplan, M.I. Posner, D.G. Stein & R.F. Thompson (Eds.), *Clinical Neuropsychology and Brain Function: Research, Measurement, and Practice*. Washington, DC: American Psychological Association.

13 Scoring and Score Tables

Once the client leaves, the focus turns to cleanup and scoring. However, as discussed later, I encourage my psychometrists to score as much as they can as they go and to use the time blocks for certain tests (e.g., while the client is completing a 15-minute math computation subtest or during a silent reading test) to score. Similarly, I encourage psychometrists to put away materials as they finish particular tests, so as to reduce the stack at the end. Consistent with our discussions of time management, the goal is to have the client's file scored and the score table generated (more on this later) by the end of the day or within 24 hours after the client is seen for testing.

Maximizing Efficiency

There is no doubt that when starting out, scoring can take as much time (or more) as test administration. Remembering where to go to find the normative tables, hand scoring based on transparent overlays, and tabulating hundreds of points by hand would take anyone a significant amount of time, particularly someone taking their time and being mindful of errors. However, we have all found ways to maximize efficiency, creating Excel scoring tables, memorizing common score conversions, and using the number keypad to hasten our speed of data entry. Technology has also advanced. For those unfamiliar with using tablets for test administration, one of the greatest benefits is the automatically generated scores at the end of each test. While there are pros and cons to these technological advancements, the efficiency they bring to scoring is a clear and undeniable benefit.

As mentioned earlier, scoring (or at minimum tabulating totals) as tests are administered is important. Even without verifying a standard score from the manual, an alarmingly low score should be brought to the neuropsychologist, as supplemental testing can then be administered based on a passing review of the subtest raw totals. I have known some psychometrists who will leave different scoring manuals open to the page where their current client's age demographic is located, allowing for a quick glance to capture the standard score shortly after administration.

DOI: 10.4324/9781003098010-14

As discussed in Chapter 8, I created a "scoring binder" while on fellowship. Working in an academic medical setting with numerous other neuropsychologists, manuals were housed in a central location convenient to everyone. Though it was surprisingly rare that a manual was taken when I needed it, I was often fatigued after testing a highly hyperactive child and didn't always feel like ending my day with repeated laps to the cabinet each time I scored a measure. As a result, I gathered the normative tables in my scoring binder so I could flip from tab to tab once my protocols were tallied. Given that many manuals are now online, the idea of the scoring binder may not be as relevant in the coming years. Nonetheless, placing labeled tabs for high-use tables or paperclipping the start of the normative table appendix can support efficient scoring. This can be a helpful resource for your psychometrist as well.

Once all of the tests are scored, most providers appreciate the creation of a score table. One of my brilliant colleagues during fellowship created a spreadsheet that transformed raw scores to standard scores and filled in the appropriate percentile rank and descriptor. I regret that I never learned how to recreate that Excel file, but if that is an option for you, I highly recommend it. It can cut down on scoring transformation mistakes and save significant time.

For those who do not have an auto-score-tabulating score table spreadsheet, an independently created text document can suffice. I tend to include the raw score, standard score, percentile, and descriptor in my tables, but this is up to your own personal preferences (*see* the Appendix for a sample of my current score table). As part of the initial training, my psychometrist and I review the ways to transform scores mathematically (e.g., how to transform a Z to a standard score), and I provide a cheat sheet with these equations, though I also provide quick-access charts for reference so that they are not forced to calculate each score individually (*see* the Appendix for a copy of both the score transformation sheet as well as the quick-access charts). Nonetheless, the transformation of scores takes time, and I know many providers who prefer to report scores as they are generated by the test's respective scoring program (e.g., a mix of T scores, Z scores, scaled scores and standard scores). Stylistically, it is completely up to you, although it is still of benefit to teach your psychometrist how to make these score transformations and to help them understand how these scores are derived.

The Intellectual Exercise

I previously touched upon the delightful auto-tabulation of scores that is generated by computerized or tablet testing. Just as the Wisconsin Card Sort Task can be administered by hand, it also can be administered (and autoscored) with the click of a button. Call me old-school, but I think it is important for a psychometrist or trainee to administer and score all tests by hand before transitioning to the computer or auto-score options. Efficiency is wonderful, but training in hand scoring is tremendously beneficial for a deeper understanding of the test, how the construct is derived, and how the score is generated. Besides, you never know when a hurricane or snowstorm is going to cause a power outage, or when the Internet might become unreliable.

Normative Samples

While most manuals provide the normative tables for raw score conversion, updated norms for specialized populations are frequently published as journal articles rather than formal manual supplements. Just as I routinely review journal articles on topics of interest, I encourage my psychometrist to review articles detailing subsample or updated normative data for the tests we routinely administer.

After Scoring: Housekeeping Basics

Once score tables are created, the psychometrist can pass the file along to the neuropsychologist for review and report writing. However, I ask my psychometrist to review all documents in the file, placing identification labels on each form (e.g., a label that includes the clients name, date of birth, date of visit, and a place to initial for the person who administered the test). This way, if a client's file falls off of my desk, or even worse, two files fall off my desk simultaneously, all pages are identified as part of the individual client's file. I initially asked the psychometrist to place identification labels on protocols *before* testing began but found that with no-shows and last-minute cancelations, this often resulted in wasted time (and stickers). Therefore, stickering the file can occur while the client is testing, but I ask that it be completed before the file is brought to me.

Once the client's report is written, I return the file to my psychometrist for processing. The psychometrist breaks down the file, scanning all protocols onto a secure server and shredding the original forms. In this way, we reduce the amount of paper in the office, and we are able to easily access raw data of clients if needed. While larger academic medical settings may have dedicated staff people to process files after they are complete, this is often a very straightforward and simple task for a psychometrist to complete. I've had some psychometrist describe it as "the Zen part" of their day.

Reference

Guilmette, T.J., Sweet, J.J., Hebben, N., Koltai, D., Mahone, E.M., Spiegler, B.J., . . . Conference Participants. (2020). American academy of clinical neuropsychology consensus conference statement on uniform labeling of performance test scores. *The Clinical Neuropsychologist, 34*(3), 437–453.

14 Diverse Populations

Unique Considerations

It would take a multivolume work to explore all of the unique characteristics to consider when assessing diverse individuals. Encouragingly, there is a recent push for critical self-examination, and the ways we interact with, assess, and interpret results from individuals from ethnoracially, culturally, and linguistically diverse backgrounds (*see* Cory, 2021). There is also ongoing attention to and discussion around the impacts of sensory impairment or physical disability on testing methods and interpretation across the life span. Further, there is a bourgeoning area of research with lesbian, bisexual, gay, transgender, queer, intersex, and asexual (LGBTQIA) populations. For example, gender identity and appropriate normative group selection, or impacts of hormone therapy on neurocognitive abilities (two of many pertinent examples), are being thoughtfully discussed in clinical arenas and systematically explored in research.

The following is a brief compilation of supplemental resources aimed at deepening understanding and broaching the conversations of cultural competence across a select set of diverse groups. This list of groups is far from exhaustive, and I implore neuropsychologists to support the education of their psychometrists, inclusive of whatever populations are dominant within one's practice or academic setting. A more intensive, supplemental discussion can be reengaged closer to the time when a patient requiring a specific support (e.g., someone who is hearing impaired requiring the use of a frequency modulation [FM] system) is scheduled for testing. However, discussions of broader cultural competence are complex and should be ongoing, and I would encourage involvement of psychometry team members in routinely held professional didactics aimed at enhancing competence across diverse populations.

The ethics and standards chapters of this book (Chapters 5 and 6) provide insight into testing accommodations and modifications for various types of populations. I again encourage neuropsychologists to have their psychometrists review both ethical guidelines and assessment standards regarding diverse individuals.

The resources listed here comprise three to five relevant, representative publications at the time of the book's publication. This is an evolving area of

DOI: 10.4324/9781003098010-15

research and reflection, so readers are encouraged to use these references as starting points and as resources for finding updated resources on the subjects.

I will also note that while there are many studies that discuss the *interpretation* of assessment data in the context of diverse populations and conditions, as it pertains to psychometrists, it is important to discuss the ways these factors impact and interact with the *testing* process. Therefore, psychometrists' training should be focused on their individual contribution to the testing experience of clients (e.g., using appropriate pronouns for transgender clients, speaking directly to the client when working with an interpreter, understanding the possible experience of the patient if the psychometrist is from a different racial/ethnic/cultural group), and vice versa.

As mentioned in the following sections, at times accommodations or modifications must be provided to support an individual's ability to demonstrate knowledge in a particular area. The following definitions are provided for context, as often I have observed accommodation and modification used interchangeably when describing methods of increasing accessibility:

- **Accommodation:** an alteration to the environment or format that allows an individual with a disability to gain access to opportunities to demonstrate knowledge on a particular construct or constructs. It does not alter content, just the individual's ability to access said content. It can include modifying test format, response format or timing (Hill-Briggs et al., 2007)
- **Modification:** a change to content, thus altering the information that is presented. Often, when modification is necessary, there is no normative data for the modified version. Thus, modifications most often negate or severely limit the conclusions that can be drawn from the normative data provided by the test publisher or otherwise.
- **Accessibility:** test takers should be given an unobstructed opportunity to demonstrate their standing on the construct(s) being measured. Accessible testing means all test takers are able to show their status on a target construct(s) without being unduly advantaged or disadvantaged by an individual characteristic or characteristics. (American Educational Research Association, American Psychological Association, & National Council on Measurement in Education, 2014).

It is critically important to actively listen, acknowledge, think critically, and act intently when interacting with and assessing individuals of the same and different backgrounds as our own. I strive to educate myself across these areas, recognizing that I have gaps in knowledge and areas for improvement. Within that context, I share here some of the resources that I've found helpful in educating myself and in training psychometrists who are assessing individuals from diverse populations. Included in each section is a compilation of book chapters and articles, in hopes that the resources send you on your own journey toward promoting psychometrist competence in assessing the diverse clients of your practice, clinic, or department. These lists are by no means exhaustive; they simply offer a starting point.

Cultural, Racial, Ethnic, and Linguistically Diverse Populations

Issues of cultural, racial, ethnic, and linguistic diversity should be thoughtfully considered for each patient seen for assessment. From a testing perspective, psychometrists are urged to reflect upon their own identity and to discuss the possible impact their own identity has on the testing experience of their clients. Further, discussions around appropriate normative data sets for diverse groups are important in the training of psychometrists, as often the normative group of the client is not adequately represented in normative data provided by test publishers. While it is primarily the duty of the neuropsychologist to provide a test list to psychometrists, it can be instructive for a psychometrist to consider how different tests may unfairly disadvantage certain cultural groups, or have an understanding as to why certain groups may appear to have more perceived "difficulty" on certain tasks (e.g., lack of exposure to certain words).

Byrd, D.A., Rivera Mindt, M.M., Clark, U.S., Clarke, Y., Thames, A.D., Gammada, E.Z., & Manly, J.J. (2021). Creating an antiracist psychology by addressing professional complicity in psychological assessment. *Psychological Assessment, 33*(3), 279–285.

Cory, J.M. (2021). White privilege in neuropsychology: An 'invisible knapsack' in need of unpacking? *The Clinical Neuropsychologist, 35*(2), 206–218.

Fugi, D.E.M. (2018). Developing a cultural context for conducting a neuropsychological evaluation with a culturally diverse client: The ECLECTIC framework. *The Clinical Neuropsychologist, 32*(8), 1356–1392.

Rabin, L.A., Brodale, D.L., Elbulok-Charcape, M.M., & Barr, W.B. (2019). Challenges in the neuropsychological assessment of ethnic minorities. *Clinical Cultural Neuroscience: An Integrative Approach to Cross-Cultural Neuropsychology*, 55–81.

Rivera Mindt, M., Byrd, D., Saez, P., & Manly, J. (2010). Increasing culturally competent neuropsychological services for ethnic minority populations: A call to action. *The Clinical Neuropsychologist, 24*, 429–453.

LGBTQIA Individuals

I found the article by Trittschuh and colleagues to be wonderfully instructive and clear about the considerations that are appropriate when assessing transgender individuals (2018). Many of the points made regarding asking a person how they would like to be addressed, taking care not to assume a particular gender identity based on physical characteristics or given name at birth, and again assessing the appropriateness of certain normative groups stratified by gender are valuable to consider for any LGBTQIA individual. Self-reflection around automatic assumptions (e.g., client is wearing blue and goes by the name John so they must have been born a male) and the ways we can support inclusivity while respecting individuality are excellent exercises for both psychometrists and neuropsychologists, as well as any patient-facing staff person.

Trittschuh, E.H., Parmenter, B.A., Clausell, E.R., Mariano, M.J., & Reger, M.A. (2018). Conducting neuropsychological assessment with transgender individuals. *The Clinical Neuropsychologist, 32*(8), 1393–1410.

Hawks, E.M., Holster, J., Cowperthwaite, R., Lewis, A.L., Hart, J., & Ostermeyer, B.K. (2019). Psychological assessment and treatment for LGBTQ+ patients. *Psychiatric Annals, 49*(10), 436–440.

Clients With Visual Impairment or Blindness

Neuropsychologists and psychometrists face a host of challenges when assessing individuals with visual impairment or blindness (VI/B). While there are some tests that do not require the viewing of visual stimuli, they are rare and do not always fully capture the abilities of an individual with VI/B. Further, there are both congenital and acquired etiologies for VI/B, expanding the heterogeneity of the population and muddying the waters when it comes to assigning appropriate normative groups for various tests. It is further challenging to gather sufficient normative data for each subset of individuals experiencing VI/B, and thus appropriate normative data may not be readily available. From a testing perspective, psychometrists frequently working with individuals with VI/B should be trained in a variety of accommodations for individuals with VI/B, including the use of large print or braille documents, accommodations such as hand-over-hand modeling for appropriate tasks, and oral administration of tests when verbal responses are acceptable.

Decker, S.L., Strait, J.E., Roberts, A.M., & Ferraracci, J. (2018). Intellectual and neuropsychological assessment of individuals with sensory and physical disabilities and traumatic brain injury. In D.P. Flanagan & E.M. McDonough (Eds.), *Contemporary Intellectual Assessment: Theories, Tests, and Issues* (pp. 662–683). The Guilford Press.

Gallagher, J.T., & Burnham, K.A. (2017). *Neuropsychological Assessment of Adults with Visual Impairment*. Stoelting.

Sattler, J., & Evans, C.A. (2006). Visual impairments. In J. Sattler & R. Hoge (Eds.), *Assessment of Children: Behavioral, Social, and Clinical Foundations* (5th Ed., pp. 367–376). San Diego, CA: Sattler Publishing.

Clients With Hearing Impairment or Deafness

Another unique population is individuals with hearing impairment or deafness (HI/D). Testing with these individuals often requires accommodation for communication, including the use of an interpreter who can convey information through sign language. Once again, there is extensive linguistic diversity in the deaf community, and thus it is optimal to find an interpreter fluent in the communication mode of the client. For those psychometrists who frequently work with individuals with HI/D, supplemental training in the use of FM monitors or other volume-enhancing methods, the use of supplemental written instructions, when appropriate, or the experience of testing with the assistance of an interpreter is essential. Fortunately, there seems to be an extensive literature regarding assessment of individuals with HI/B.

Beck, D.L., & Harvey, M. (2021). Issues in cognition, audiology and amplification. *Hearing Review, 28*(1), 28–33.

Sattler, J., Hardy-Braz, S.T., & Willis, J.O. (2006). Hearing impairments. In J. Sattler & R. Hoge (Eds.), *Assessment of Children: Behavioral, Social, and Clinical Foundations* (5th Ed., pp. 478–492). San Diego, CA: Sattler Publishing.

Völter, C., Götze, L., Dazert, S., Wirth, R., & Thomas, J.P. (2020). Impact of hearing loss on geriatric assessment. *Clinical Interventions in Aging, 15*, 2453.

Wong, C.G., Rapport, L.J., Stach, B.A., & Ramachandran, V. (2020). Effect of age-related hearing loss on neuropsychological test performance. *The Hearing Journal, 73*(3), 16–17.

Clients With Physical Disabilities

Physical disability is an area of notably few assessment-framed articles, although it is likely that information is contained in articles that discuss testing of particular populations (e.g., cerebral palsy, stroke) who more frequently experience physical disability. Nonetheless, if a client arrives with dense hemiparesis from a stroke or was born with severe cerebral palsy, it is expected that reasonable accommodations for motor difficulties will be provided during testing. Similar to sensory impairments, physical disabilities can result from many different congenital or acquired conditions, and unless the assessment is meant to quantify the extent to which the physical disability impacts performance on a task (e.g., a right-hand fine motor task given to quantify fine motor impairment in an individual who suffered a left middle cerebral artery stroke), reasonable accommodations should be made to support the individual. When conceptualizing psychometrists' training in this area, consideration around the tests for which the psychometrist could complete the motor task for the client based on his or her verbal feedback, oral administration of appropriate tasks, the utilization of pencil grips, slant boards, document holders, wrist weights, or otherwise to facilitate client-initiated responses, and others are all topics worthy of time and thoughtful consideration. As with all other accommodations made, training around the importance of documenting any changes so the neuropsychologist can interpret scores appropriately is critical.

The psychometrist should also be trained to consider space limitations and the overall office setup when preparing to assess an individual with a physical disability. Ensuring there is sufficient room for an individual in a wheelchair to maneuver in and out of the testing space, verifying that the height of the test table is high enough so the individual in a wheelchair can easily wheel up to close to the edge of the table, and planning for sufficient rest breaks to address needs for weight shifting or position changes are important. It is possible that due to pain or fatigue, shorter, repeated testing sessions may be required.

Decker, S.L., Strait, J.E., Roberts, A.M., & Ferraracci, J. (2018). Intellectual and neuropsychological assessment of individuals with sensory and physical disabilities and traumatic brain injury. In D.P. Flanagan & E.M. McDonough (Eds.), *Contemporary Intellectual Assessment: Theories, Tests, and Issues* (pp. 662–683). The Guilford Press.

Hill-Briggs, F., Dial, J.G., Morere, D.A., & Joyce, A. (2007). Neuropsychological assessment of persons with physical disability, visual impairment or blindness, and hearing impairment or deafness. *Archives of Clinical Neuropsychology*, *22*(3), 389–404.

Non-native Language Speakers and Translated Tests: Working With Interpreters

When working with an interpreter, there are many added layers to the testing process. First, it is critical that the interpreter arrives with adequate time to discuss the process of testing with the psychometrist. Often translators working in larger medical centers have familiarity with translating standardized assessments, but it is ideal if communication with the interpreter can begin a few days before the client is tested. In this way, the neuropsychologist, psychometrist, and interpreter can work together to identify if there are particular measures already translated into the client's native language, thereby reducing the amount of "on the spot" translation the interpreter needs to do. It also can be extremely helpful for the interpreter to review the specific measures to be administered, as often there are not exact, one-to-one translations of certain words. Once the measures are selected and the battery is reviewed, further conversations can be had regarding the testing process itself.

It is important to review general etiquette with the psychometrist (e.g., talk directly to the patient (not to the translator), keeping eye contact with the patient as if we were speaking the same language). It may be helpful to share pointers such as speaking slightly slower or pausing more frequently to allow the interpreter to convey the information the psychometrist said to the client.

When reviewing the process of testing with the interpreter, it is critical that the individual translate exactly what the psychometrist says, and vice versa. I discuss the importance of telling me *exactly* what the patient says, even if the interpreter doesn't think it is correct or feels the client isn't making sense. In the same way, I tell the interpreter that they must not provide any supplemental explanations or deviate from translating the words I say in any way. If the client requests clarification, I ask the translator to tell me, and if it is permissible, I provide an alternative method for explaining the directions. Throughout, documentation around difficulties with translation, confusion, or instances where the translation may not be exact must be noted.

For tasks such as a verbal list learning task, the interpreter does not repeat after me but instead reads the entire list while I observe. Prior to administration, I discuss the importance of pacing and either writing down or telling me the exact words the client says as they say them and the importance of telling me the words in the same order as the client. While most interpreters are very good and understand the reasons for this level of strictness, it can nonetheless be helpful to provide the interpreter with rationale for adherence to standardization prior to working with the client. As mentioned previously, a team approach, including psychometrist, neuropsychologist, and interpreter, will likely result in obtaining the best possible data from the client.

Bolaños-Medina, A., & González-Ruiz, V. (2012). Deconstructing the translation of psychological tests. *Meta: Journal des Traducteurs/Meta: Translators' Journal*, *57*(3), 715–739.

Casas, R., Guzmán-Vélez, E., Cardona-Rodriguez, J., Rodriguez, N., Quiñones, G., Izaguirre, B., & Tranel, D. (2012). Interpreter-mediated neuropsychological testing of monolingual Spanish speakers. *The Clinical Neuropsychologist*, *26*(1), 88–101.

Forensic Clients

Increasingly, neuropsychologists are providing expert consultation to legal teams by evaluating individuals in the midst of litigation. It is important to provide supplemental training to a psychometrist involved in forensic evaluations, noting a few critical details. While it should go without saying, all clients are treated with the utmost respect, even if they are felt to be misrepresenting, exaggerating, or mischaracterizing their difficulties. There is never a time when it is appropriate to point out discrepancies (e.g., client required a cane to walk into the testing room but did not think to use it when excusing him or herself to the restroom) or to convey to the client in any way that the psychometrist has any judgments about the validity of his or her performance on testing.

It is further important to consider that the individual sitting in front of the psychometrist is not the client of the neuropsychologist. Thus, while there are no changes to standardized administration, there is not the typical relationship whereby the neuropsychologist will provide feedback to the client. Therefore, psychometrists should be made aware that if questions about performance arise, it is important to direct the client to his or her legal counsel or insurance company. Additionally, for forensic clients who later call requesting feedback or results, no information is provided, and they are again directed to their lawyer or insurance provider. That final note is for psychometrists who also act in an office manager/staff capacity, or who may answer the phone if a client calls. The testing process, beyond expected increases in performance validity tests (PVTs) and symptom validity tests (SVTs), should otherwise look the same.

While I have yet to come across any chapters specifically discussing the testing process with forensic clients (again due to the likelihood that it would not look significantly different than other testing clients), I nonetheless find the following texts helpful for context:

Boone, K.B. (2012). *Clinical Practice of Forensic Neuropsychology: An Evidence-Based Approach*. New York: Guilford Press.

Bush, S.S., Demakis, G.J., & Rohling, M.L. (2017). *APA Handbook of Forensic Neuropsychology*. American Psychological Association.

Morgan, J.E., & Ricker, J.H. (Eds.). (2018). *Textbook of Clinical Neuropsychology*. New York: Taylor & Francis.

Sherman, E.M.S., & Brooks, B.L. (2012). *Pediatric Forensic Neuropsychology*. New York: Oxford University Press.

Pediatric Clients

Pediatric clients are not simply miniature adults, and thus if you are a pediatric neuropsychologist you are already well aware of the unique challenges children can pose in the testing setting. While other chapters in this book review behavioral management strategies and methods to enhance compliance with testing, it may nonetheless be beneficial to support your psychometrist's understanding of topics such as normal development (e.g., "is it appropriate that the child is reversing letters at this age, or should I note it in behavioral observations?") or considerations around ways children may uniquely engage in the testing experience (e.g., "should I allow the child to use the restroom again if he just used the facilities three minutes ago?").

Anderson, V., Northam, E., Hendy, J., & Wrennall, J. (2019). *Developmental Neuropsychology: A Clinical Approach*. New York: Routledge.

Baron, I.S. (2018). *Neuropsychological Evaluation of the Child: Domains, Methods, & Case Studies*. New York: Oxford University Press.

Olson, K., & Jacobson, K. (2015). Cross cultural considerations in pediatric neuropsychology: A review and call to action. *Applied Neuropsychology: Child, 4*, 166–177.

Morgan, J.E., & Ricker, J.H. (Eds.). (2018). *Textbook of Clinical Neuropsychology*. New York: Taylor & Francis.

Geriatric Clients

In a similar way to pediatrics, geriatric clients warrant special consideration in the testing setting. Given the known changes to hearing and vision, for example, psychometrists primarily working in a geriatric setting may benefit from training on various sensory-enhancing options (e.g., FM monitor, use of a magnifying glass or sheet to enhance text) or on considerations around safety (e.g., sitting for a while may increase the possibility of unsteadiness upon standing), among other things. Discussions around how to respond to clients with clear memory difficulties (e.g., asking the same question repeatedly) or frustrations with family members who "forced" or "tricked" them into coming for testing would also be beneficial. It is possible that an older adult client may require more frequent rest breaks if they happen to be taking certain types of medication or that they may need support remembering to put on their glasses prior to engaging in visually based testing.

Bush, S., & Martin, T.A. (Eds.). (2005). *Geriatric Neuropsychology: Practice Essentials*. New York: Taylor & Francis.

McPherson, S., & Koltai, D. (2018). *A Practical Guide to Geriatric Neuropsychology*. New York: Oxford University Press.

Ravdin, L., & Katzen, H. (Eds.). (2019). *Handbook on the Neuropsychology of Aging and Dementia* (2nd Ed.). New York: Springer.

Veterans

Though I have not personally worked in a VA or military setting, survey results emphasized the importance of understanding military culture, lingo, and structure as an important component of a psychometrist's training if they work on a military base or in a VA setting. Here is a compilation of recent work around military culture, with some articles specifically focused on cultural and ethical considerations in training programs.

Atuel, H.R., & Castro, C.A. (2018). Military cultural competence. *Clinical Social Work Journal*, *46*(2), 74–82.

Cole, R.F. (2014). Understanding military culture: A guide for professionals and school counselors. *Professional Counselor*, *4*(5), 497–504.

Goldenberg, M., Hamaoka, D., Santiago, P., & McCarroll, J. (2012). *Basic Training: A Primer on Military Life and Culture for Health Care Providers*. Bethesda, MD.

Meyer, E.G., Writer, B.W., & Brim, W. (2016). The importance of Military cultural competence. *Current Psychiatry Reports*, *18*(26), 1–8.

Strom, T.Q., Gavian, M.E., Possis, E., Loughlin, J., Bui, T., Linardatos, E . . . Siegel, W. (2012). Cultural and ethical considerations when working with military personnel and veterans: A primer for VA training programs. *Training and Education in Professional Psychology*, *6*(2), 67–75.

Conclusions

In closing, I hope this chapter facilitates ongoing critical consideration and robust discussion about the unique individuals who pass through our doors each day. Tailoring psychometrists' training to groups of clients most frequently seen in a practice, department, or clinic is essential and can assist the psychometrist in helping you provide the best possible care to your patients.

References

American Educational Research Association, American Psychological Association, & National Council on Measurement in Education (Eds.). (2014). *Standards for Educational and Psychological Testing*. Washington, DC: American Educational Research Association.

Baron, I.S. (2018). *Neuropsychological Evaluation of the Child: Domains, Methods, & Case Studies*. New York: Oxford University Press.

Hill-Briggs, F., Dial, J.G., Morere, D.A., & Joyce, A. (2007). Neuropsychological assessment of persons with physical disability, visual impairment or blindness, and hearing impairment or deafness. *Archives of Clinical Neuropsychology*, *22*(3), 389–404.

Taylor, D.M. (2018). Americans with disabilities: 2014. *US Census Bureau Current Population Reports*, 70–152.

15 Supplemental Responsibilities in Various Settings

Diverse Settings

This chapter includes some of the supplemental responsibilities and expectations commonly requested of psychometrists in various settings.

Supplemental Responsibilities

Inventory and Ordering of Testing Supplies and Equipment

While likely common across settings, psychometrists are often asked to maintain some form of supply inventory for test protocols and response booklets. It often falls to them to order replacement forms as the need arises and to keep tabs on the state of more frequently used stimulus books and equipment. If inventory needs remain relatively stable and are well-tracked across a lengthier period of time (about one year), it can be possible to do a large order around the time of one of our many international conferences in order to take advantage of test publishers' discount codes offered to conference attendees. While it can be challenging to predict all assessment needs and may be particularly difficult if a new edition of a test is anticipated, tracking inventory can still amount to significant cost savings and can be a worthwhile supplemental request for your psychometrist.

Ordering Office Supplies

It is not uncommon to supplement a psychometrist's daily duties with office managerial or clerical tasks, particularly in the private practice setting. Just as psychometrists are often asked to maintain inventory of testing supplies and other assessment necessities, psychometrists in private practice may also be asked to order routine supplies such as notepads, materials for a coffee or beverage station, paper, printer ink, or other general office needs. Asking the psychometrist to keep a spreadsheet or log of these costs can be an added benefit, as it allows the private practitioner to get a sense of office operational costs.

DOI: 10.4324/9781003098010-16

Answering Phones

Psychometrists are often best qualified to answer the phone and explain to clients the process and procedures of a neuropsychological evaluation. New psychometrists may benefit from a phone script or a specific set of practice-specific questions to ask potential clients. For those cases that are more complicated, a system can be set up with your psychometrist to allow you to make return calls and assess the fit of the client to your practice. For those more straightforward cases, psychometrists can quickly explain the process of a neuropsychological evaluation, what to expect on the testing day, provide your typical report-turnaround timeframe, and answer questions the client raises (e.g., "does your practice participate in insurance?"). Particularly when provided with a structured form with specific questions to ask, psychometrists are quite qualified to step into this role.

Scheduling Clients

Psychometrists in a private practice may also take the lead on scheduling clients and preparing the necessary pre-evaluation paperwork. In many practices, printed letters and questionnaires have now been replaced with a follow-up email, confirming the date and time of the appointment and providing links to various questionnaires to complete. Reminder emails can be automatically generated or sent by the psychometrist a few days in advance or, if requested paperwork is not completed, by a prespecified date.

Maintaining Clinic Schedules

In large academic medical centers, psychometrists often are tasked with the responsibility of maintaining and creating clinic schedules. The lead psychometrist assigns the different psychometrists to each neuropsychologist, many on a rotating basis, and the same individual is quickly able to step in and make changes if a client doesn't arrive or if there is a last-minute cancellation.

Insurance Preauthorization or Verification

In speaking with colleagues, it appears that the vast majority of private practitioners do not take insurance. While many of us may provide an appropriately coded superbill for clients to submit after their evaluation, most are not paneled with insurance companies. Nonetheless, some practices make psychometrists available to clients to support the client's investigation of reimbursement through their insurance company. Once provided with the client's insurance information, the psychometrist can give the company a call and inquire as to the needs for preauthorization paperwork or to assist in determining the amount of reimbursement expected. As you are likely aware, this is a full-time job for many individuals in larger institutional or medical settings, because it can take up a significant amount of time. It may be more beneficial to pool together with other neuropsychologists in private practice and hire a specific individual to assist with insurance, rather than adding this to the psychometrist's list of responsibilities.

Cleaning Materials

While it is not customary to have your psychometrist fill the role of your office cleaning staff person, it may be requested that a psychometrist assist with cleaning frequently used items, particularly in the pediatric setting. For example, toys from an infant assessment should be cleaned after use, especially those that are tempting enough to enter the infant's mouth. It may be worth identifying this expectation for psychometrists if this pertains to your practice.

Mailing

For those still mailing reports and forms to families, preparing welcome packets or other mailings for clients often falls to the psychometrist in private practice. Depending on the practice or department, the psychometrist may be asked to organize routine mailings to all prior clients (e.g., newsletter updates, new services offered, introduction of a new provider who has joined the team), or to simply prepare and send reports as they are completed.

Scanning

Despite a desire to reduce paper waste, physical forms and answer booklets may forever be a component of our assessment procedures. Thus, a psychometrist can be asked to scan a completed file following the client's appointment in the office. It goes without saying that a system to verify that the client's electronic data are both available in case of need in the future and protected from unauthorized access is critical, but scanning the file and shredding the paper form can be the final steps in closing a client's case after the evaluation is complete.

Social Media and Outreach

Psychometrists can support the ongoing growth of a private practice setting through their engagement in strategic outreach. For example, following up with a school district to verify that a report was received and to schedule a follow-up conversation with the neuropsychologist handling the case may result in future work from that district. Similarly, dropping off pamphlets or fliers to the director of a new day care, elder care facility or private school on behalf of the practice with subsequent follow up to schedule a call with the neuropsychologist can result in a new referral source. While it is not always appropriate to send the psychometrist to complete these tasks, involvement in a multi-pronged community outreach plan can do wonders for increasing clients over time.

Client Spreadsheets for Research and Follow Up

Particularly in pediatrics, it is often recommended that a client be reevaluated after a certain period of time. Psychometrists can be asked to input pertinent information into a spreadsheet or database that allows for tracking and reminders when the client is ready to be contacted for reevaluation. Life gets busy for all of us, and families certainly appreciate the check-in and willingness of the practice to reach out and inquire as to the need for a reevaluation one to two years after their initial appointment. This benefits everyone, as you are able to repeat batteries and complete comparative analyses to support the ongoing success of your client, and it helps the families feel cared for and supported.

If there is documentation in your consent forms regarding the future use of data for research purposes, information can be inputted into a spreadsheet or database for future research analysis. This can be particularly beneficial if you also supervise graduate students seeking data for research projects or dissertations, as well as for your ongoing ability to present work at national and international conferences.

Billing and Time Documentation

There are some hospitals that require psychometrists to create a patient encounter and to file billing charges on the date of the evaluation. While the neuropsychologist typically signs off on these, it is possible that a psychometrist would be asked to create the initial encounter or document testing in an electronic medical record.

Training of Trainees: Interns, Externs, or Postdoctoral Fellows

More often in academic training facilities, there is some level of expectation that the psychometrist work closely with trainees to ensure maintenance of standardized procedures or to teach them new or unfamiliar tests. This may not be written into a formal calendar or set time, but there may be an assumed expectation that the psychometrist be available to answer questions, demonstrate administration, or practice with trainees when not engaged in testing.

Multidisciplinary Team Engagement

While it is the neuropsychologist who provides treatment planning support and recommendations to a multidisciplinary team, psychometrists working in multidisciplinary settings may have to coordinate testing around other therapies, book shorter blocks of time around previously set schedules, and assist nurses or other medical care providers as to the needs of the patient during testing. For example, while it seems quite possible to draw blood during the second trial of a verbal list learning task, there are reasons why this is discouraged, and the psychometrist should be made aware of their need to coordinate care and advocate for the patient's ability to complete the verbal memory task prior to blood draw in these moments.

Research Coordination or Involvement

Finally, there are some psychometrists who are involved in research coordination or the running of research participants for various studies. I am aware of some sites where psychometrists are trained in a specific therapeutic intervention program or a highly specific research protocol and may be engaged in various research processes and procedures. This could include maintaining an institutional review board filing, running of participants, data entry, or support for analysis of participant data.

Concluding Remarks

No matter what the task is, the most frequent comment made by psychometrists on the surveys was that they wanted to feel like a member of a team rather than a cog in the wheel or a "workhorse." While we have all been asked to do tasks that are menial, boring, or we do not feel adequately reflect our experience, there are instances in which these tasks arise. Consider the experience of the psychometrist when you request that they complete such tasks. Consider acknowledging that this task is perhaps not formally within their job description, and verbalize your appreciation for their willingness to support the team by completing it. Appreciation and mutual respect will enhance the office climate for all those working there.

16 Promoting Best Practices by Supporting Psychometrists' Continuing Education

As clinical psychologists, we complete continuing education credits to demonstrate our commitment to keeping up with professional advancements in our field. As clinical neuropsychologists who have completed the board certification process, we further agree to complete trainings consistent with expected maintenance of certification (MOC) requirements. We work in an exciting and rapidly evolving field, where advancements in assessment techniques, medicine, therapeutics, neuroscience, neuroimaging, and others are expanding at such a rapid rate that it can make it tough to keep up. Nonetheless, we commit to keeping up with as much as we can. In the same way, we are tasked with instilling the value of lifelong learning and professional knowledge growth in those who work under our license. From trainees to psychometrists, it is our job to promote acquisition of knew knowledge and skills. I want to touch upon some of the methods by which we can support ongoing training. While this is not meant to be an exhaustive list nor a checklist of requirements, my hope is that some of these opportunities will fit within your current practice or institutional framework, and can be implemented and fine-tuned as needed.

Leading by Example

This one may seem fairly obvious, but we must begin with ourselves. Requirements for continuing education and MOC are one reason that we choose to seek out new training, but it is also because we have a natural curiosity and excitement for our rapidly growing field. With diverse experiences, topics, and opportunities, there are endless opportunities to dig deep into a topic of interest. If we cultivate this excitement, interest, and desire for growth attainment in our trainees and psychometrists, we are setting the stage for naturally occurring discussion, debate, advancement, and enhancement within our own practice walls.

Didactics and Ongoing Training Seminars

In connecting with the many contributors to this book, I learned that there are diverse ways that practices and institutions conduct didactic and

DOI: 10.4324/9781003098010-17

professional development series. Some institutions provide quarterly professional development rounds whereby psychometrists join neuropsychologists to review new articles, discuss departmental policies and procedures, or review frequently used tests. I am aware of others who have psychometry meetings every Friday afternoon, during which all psychometrists come together to discuss cases or review tests. Yet a third option is an all-day, testing recalibration boot-camp that quite frankly sounds like a lot of fun! Whatever your preferred method may be, I encourage the inclusion of psychometrists in this ongoing training and these professional development opportunities.

Conference or Training Attendance

Along the lines of professional development, psychometrists may be interested in attending conferences (NAP hosts their conference at the same time and in the same city as the International Neuropsychology Society (INS) conference) or opportunities to attend trainings for newly published tests. The NAP conference is an excellent way for psychometrists to build community, network, and learn about new advancements in testing. Particularly if you attend INS, the psychometrist can't be seeing patients without you there; thus if your budget allows, plan to provide support for attendance at this, or perhaps a different, more local or relevant conference.

Board Certification in Psychometry

While there were rather conflicted responses to questions around board certification in psychometry from neuropsychologist survey respondents (see Chapter 2), if your psychometrist is interested, it may be worth engaging in a conversation around support for their joining of NAP or engaging in the Board Certification in Psychometry (BCP) process. Many psychometrists who responded to the survey had completed their board certification and shared that they found it of benefit for both professional and financial reasons.

Structured Goal Setting

Another take away from the psychometry survey was frustration around the lack of perceived upward mobility in psychometry. I think it can be helpful to set clear, attainable goals each year with your psychometrist—perhaps, it is involvement in a book review or a goal to update your practice or department-specific psychometry training handbook. If they attend the NAP conference discussed earlier, perhaps support their submission to present a poster or give a talk. Whatever it is, being able to support the growth of your psychometrist during their time working with you is quite rewarding.

Wise Words of Advice to New Psychometrists From Current Psychometrists

When asked for the "one piece of advice" current psychometrists would share with new psychometry trainees, the following gems were shared:

- Be patient with yourself when learning new assessments, and always take your time scoring. There are many different tests and it is important that you take your time to be sure your work is accurate.
- Be aware of your role as a psychometrist and be cognizant of the boundaries. Try to understand opportunities to grow within the practice or department.
- Psychometry is a skill, and practice makes perfect.
- Take the time to pour over the manuals; you'll be amazed at all the information you can learn! It will also help you to be more comfortable in the testing space when you start to work with clients.
- Testing never goes as planned. Prepare to be flexible and understanding, as the testing process can be very stressful for patients.
- Organization and advanced preparation are keys to success. There is no such thing as spending too much time organizing or preparing. This will help to minimize errors, maximize rapport and ensure that testing is as smooth and pleasant for the patient as possible.
- Because testing is so standardized it can sometimes feel robotic; rapport-building is therefore a huge necessity!
- Be thorough, and don't be afraid to ask a lot of questions, particularly before you start testing independently.
- Order of administration really matters!
- Overprepare for cases. Learn everything you can about the patient and the tests you are giving. This allows you to figure out a backup plan if something goes awry.
- Don't let yourself take on too much all at once. There are a lot of different tests and scoring methods, and it is easy to get overwhelmed if you take on too much.
- Follow standardization meticulously first, then "test the limits" so you can gather information for your supervisor to formulate a well-informed interpretation.
- Eventually you will understand and know how to do all the tests being administered, it just takes a whole lot of time and a whole lot more practice!
- Check, re-check, and check once more when initially learning to score. Take it slow, and take notes when first starting out.
- Take the time to memorize the directions for test when first starting out. This frees you up to focus on observing the patient, and taking better behavioral observations.

Work closely with your attending neuropsychologist. Don't be afraid to ask for more information about what a test measures or why certain tests are used.

PAY ATTENTION

Practice, practice, and practice some more.

Don't score when you're tired!

Never stop being curious!

Share this book with your supervising neuropsychologist! (Okay, I added that one.)

Concluding Remarks

While there are likely even more areas that could have been reviewed within the pages of this book (e.g., an entire chapter on statistics or neuroanatomy), these were not felt to be *most* important in the initial training of a psychometrist. While eventual review of disorders, diseases or the neuroanatomical bases for the behaviors observed in testing can be wonderful ways to enhance training, they are not felt to be critical to the initial training goals. Should you feel otherwise, I encourage you to include these topics in your training process from the start. Nonetheless, my hope is that this serves as a general reference to anyone who is training a psychometrist, or engaging in testing and wanting to refine their skills.

Appendix

Psychometrist Candidate Interview Form

Name: ____________________ Date of Interview: ________________

Important Facets of the Psychometrist/Office Manager Position

- Practice structure (employees, etc.)
- Patient populations and general clinic flow
- **Psychometry Duties**: administer assessments, score, summarize behavioral observations, create score tables, organize/maintain testing inventory
- **Office Management Duties**: keeping all clinical and forensic cases organized, answering phones, scheduling clients, ordering supplies (Staples, Amazon, Testing), scanning patient files, sending reports, uploading records, creating patient invoices, and so forth.
- **Professional Opportunities:**
    - Training (work with future grad students, post docs, etc.)
    - Social Media (community outreach/engagement)
    - Research/Professional (publications, etc.)

1. Tell me about your current position, duties, and expectations, and how you feel those experiences make you the ideal candidate for this position.

2. What specifically interested you about this position?

Psychometry-Specific Questions

3. What experience do you have administering psychological testing? Do you have experience with iPad administration/scoring? Can you provide a test list?

4. What energizes you more, testing or scoring?

5. What are some methods you use to manage uncooperative patients? What strategies have been helpful? What strategies have been unhelpful?

6. Describe a time when you were unable to successfully complete testing and how you handled it?

7. What personality traits make you an ideal psychometrist? (detail-oriented, perfectionistic)

8. Describe a time you disagreed with your supervising neuropsychologist.
   a. How did you handle it?
   b. What was the outcome?
   c. How did it affect your relationship with the supervisor?

General Questions

9. What do you find most challenging in your current position?

10. What do you envision will be the most challenging part of the current position?

11. How do you handle pressure/competing demands for your attention?

12. Would you consider yourself a big picture or detail-oriented individual? What is your method for organization?

13. How do you best receive feedback about performance?

14. Where do you see yourself in five years?

15. What draws you to a position in [STATE]?

Can you provide references:

1. Phone/Email: ______________________
2. Phone/Email: ______________________
3. Phone/Email: ______________________

Invite for in-person interview? ☐ YES ☐ NO ☐ CONTACT REFERENCES

Assessment of Psychometrist's Testing Experience

Name: ____________________ **Date of Review:** ____________________

0 = never administered
1 = minimal familiarity (< 10 administrations)
2 = familiarity (10–20 administrations)
3 = proficient (21 or > administrations)

Name of Test	*Administration Rank*	*Scoring Rank*	*Comments*

Approximate # of Pediatric Testing Clients: _____
Approximate # of Adult Testing Clients: _____
Approximate # of Geriatric Testing Clients: _____

Test Administration Check-Off Sheet

Test Name	*Observation(s)*	*Administration(s)*	*Final Check*

Name of Client: _______ DOB: __/__/___ DOE: __/__/___ AGE: __:__
Race: _____ Ethnicity: _____ Sex: M / F Gender: ____ Pronouns: _____
Hand: L / R Known Diagnoses: ___________________________________

Order of Administration ⋆SAMPLE⋆

Intelligence

- ☐ WISC-V

Validity

- ☐ TOMM

Verbal and Visual Memory

- ☐ CHAMP

Visuomotor

- ☐ Beery VMI
- ☐ Beery Visual Perception
- ☐ Beery Motor Coordination

Executive Functions

- ☐ D-KEFS Verbal Fluency
- ☐ D-KEFS Color Word Interference
- ☐ D-KEFS Trails 1, 2, 4
- ☐ WCST
- ☐ ACT
- ☐ CPT-2

Motor

- ☐ Grooved Pegboard

Academics

- ☐ Nelson Denny Reading Test ⋆ If in HS ⋆
- ☐ WIAT-III (select subtests)
  - ☐ Reading Comprehension
  - ☐ Math Problem-Solving
  - ☐ Word Reading

- ☐ Pseudoword Decoding
- ☐ Numerical Operations
- ☐ Spelling

Emotional/Behavioral

- ☐ BASC-3 parent and self-report

Adaptive

- ☐ Vineland-3

Patient Name:_________________
Date of Birth: ___/ ___/ _____
Date of Evaluation: ___/ ___/ _____
Chronological Age: ___ **years,** ___ **months**

Behavioral Observations

General:

- **Appearance**

Age:	younger	stated age	older			
Build:	average	thin	healthy	overweight	tall	short
Grooming:	clean	neglected	poor	adequate		
Dress:	appropriate	casual	mismatched	skimpy		

- **Physical Appearance/Adaptive Equipment** (braces, glasses, walk with a limp, posturing, etc.)

• **Eye Contact**	good	fleeting	avoidant	intense	quickly broken	
• **Affect**	euthymic	congruent	incongruent	flat	blunted	labile
• **Mood**	calm	reserved	sad	worried	irritated	excited
• **Medication Taken**	Yes	No	Unsure	N/A		
• **Eaten Breakfast**	Yes	No				

Behavior:

• **Interpersonal Style**	friendly	polite	chatty	open	reserved
	engaged	quiet	disengaged	annoyed	
• **Attitude**	cooperative	willing	responsive	guarded	passive
• **Approach**	cooperative	thoughtful	motivated	lethargic	impulsive
	careless	hurried	self-doubting	hesitant	
• **Arousal**	alert	clouded	drowsy	stuporous	

Attention: well-sustained inconsistent fleeting distractible hyper-alert

---

Processing Speed: appropriate reduced hyper/rushed

Efficiency: organized thoughtful disorganized impulsive inconsistent

---

Executive Functioning: focused deliberate methodical self-aware flexible disinhibited disorganized disinterested distractible hyperactive impulsive perseverative

- **Initiation:** appropriate impulsive required prompting
- **Self-monitoring:** mindful unaware aware but unable to shift approach
- **Approach to Task:** planful indifferent perfectionistic impulsive

---

Speech/Language:

- **Expression** converses easily responds to direct questions unresponsive
  - o **Fluency** easily generated reduced
  - o **Intelligibility** clear reduced slurred unintelligible
  - o **Rate** appropriate slow rapid jolting
  - o **Organization** logical tangential disorganized nonsensical
- **Receptive** Understands directions Repetition of instructions Short concrete instructions
- **Prosody** appropriate flat incongruent
- **Word-Finding Difficulties** Yes No
- **Paraphasias/Circumlocutions** Yes No

Motor Functioning:

- **Handedness** Right Left Ambidextrous
- **Ambulation** independent balance difficulties poor coordination weakness (L/R)
- **Pencil Grip** palmer dynamic tripod mature weak
- **Tremors Noted** Yes No Resting Intention

Social Functioning/Emotion/Reactivity:

- **Separation from Family:** easily required encouragement distressed
- **Engagement:** easily quiet whiney hyper (difficult to cut off)
- **Response to Feedback:** flexible frustrated meltdown anger avoidant
- **Effort:** consistent required feedback/praise inconsistent lacking

---

Behavior Management:

- **Took Significant Breaks** Yes No
- **Required Ongoing Redirection** Yes No
- **Responsive to Verbal Praise** Yes No
- **Responsive to Tangible Rewards** Yes No
- **Required Visual Schedules** Yes No

Other Noteworthy General Behavioral Observations:

** SAMPLE TEST REVIEW FORM**

NAME OF TEST

Age Range: _____-_____
Approximate Time to Complete: ______
Delay? ☐ No ☐ Yes: ________ minutes

TEST OBJECTIVE
(This test measures)

ADMINISTRATION (Note instructions here)

HINTS/TIPS
(Helpful administration hints here)

SCORING
Score Table Is Located/Scoring Program Is:

Norms/Special Populations/Special Considerations:

Process: (Note scoring directions here)

Materials Needed

Stimulus Book | Response Form

Timer | Pencil

Computer/ Tablet | Manipulatives

Other:

BEHAVIORAL OBSERVATION NOTES
(Note particular behaviors to be particularly mindful of during this test, etc.)

SCORE CONVERSION FORMULAS

Raw Score → Z SCORE → Standard Score for UNTIMED TASKS

$$\frac{\text{(Raw Score} - \text{Mean Score).}}{\text{Stand. Dev.}} = \textbf{Z SCORE}$$

(Z Score × 15) + 100 = **STANDARD SCORE**

Raw Score → Z Score → Standard Score for TIMED TASKS. ⋆Timed tasks are "mean," so mean goes first!⋆

$$\frac{\text{(Mean Score} - \text{Raw Score).}}{\text{Stand. Dev.}} = \textbf{Z SCORE}$$

(Z Score × 15) + 100 = **STANDARD SCORE**

Z Score → T Score

(Z Score × 10) + 50 = **T SCORE**

NOTE: There are also score conversion tables included in the psychometry training binder. Those are easier when there is less time to do the math!

Score Conversion Chart

Standard Score	*T Score*	*Scaled Score*	*Z Score*	*Percentile*	*Standard Descriptor*
19				<0.01	Exceptionally Low
20				<0.01	Exceptionally Low
21				<0.01	Exceptionally Low
22				<0.01	Exceptionally Low
23				<0.01	Exceptionally Low
24				<0.01	Exceptionally Low
25				<0.01	Exceptionally Low
26				<0.01	Exceptionally Low
27				<0.01	Exceptionally Low
28				<0.01	Exceptionally Low
29				<0.01	Exceptionally Low
30				<0.01	Exceptionally Low
31				<0.01	Exceptionally Low
32				<0.01	Exceptionally Low
33				<0.01	Exceptionally Low
34				<0.01	Exceptionally Low
35				<0.01	Exceptionally Low
36				<0.01	Exceptionally Low
37				<0.01	Exceptionally Low
38				<0.01	Exceptionally Low
39				<0.01	Exceptionally Low
40	10		−4	<0.01	Exceptionally Low
41	11		−3.93	<0.01	Exceptionally Low
42	11.5		−3.86	<0.01	Exceptionally Low
43	12		−3.8	<0.01	Exceptionally Low
44	12.5		−3.73	<0.01	Exceptionally Low
45	13		−3.65	0.01	Exceptionally Low
46	14		−3.6	0.02	Exceptionally Low
47	14.5		−3.55	0.02	Exceptionally Low
48	15		−3.5	0.03	Exceptionally Low
48	15.5		−3.45	0.03	Exceptionally Low
49	16		−3.4	0.03	Exceptionally Low
50	16.5		−3.35	0.04	Exceptionally Low
51	17		−3.3	0.05	Exceptionally Low

Standard Score	*T Score*	*Scaled Score*	*Z Score*	*Percentile*	*Standard Descriptor*
51	17.5		−3.25	0.05	Exceptionally Low
52	18		−3.2	0.1	Exceptionally Low
53	18.5		−3.15	0.1	Exceptionally Low
54	19	1	−3.1	0.1	Exceptionally Low
54	19.5	1	−3.05	0.1	Exceptionally Low
55	20	1	−3	0.1	Exceptionally Low
56	20.5	1	−2.95	0.1	Exceptionally Low
57	21	1	−2.9	0.2	Exceptionally Low
57	21.5	1	−2.85	0.2	Exceptionally Low
58	22	2	−2.8	0.3	Exceptionally Low
59	22.5	2	−2.75	0.3	Exceptionally Low
60	23	2	−2.7	0.4	Exceptionally Low
60	23.5	2	−2.65	0.4	Exceptionally Low
61	24	2	−2.6	0.5	Exceptionally Low
62	24.5	3	−2.55	1	Exceptionally Low
63	25	3	−2.5	1	Exceptionally Low
63	25.5	3	−2.45	1	Exceptionally Low
64	26	3	−2.4	1	Exceptionally Low
65	26.5	3	−2.35	1	Exceptionally Low
66	27	3	−2.3	1	Exceptionally Low
66	27.5	3	−2.25	1	Exceptionally Low
67	28	3	−2.2	1	Exceptionally Low
68	28.5	4	−2.15	2	Exceptionally Low
69	29	4	−2.1	2	Exceptionally Low
69	29.5	4	−2.05	2	Exceptionally Low
70	30	4	−2	2	Below Average
71	30.5	4	−1.95	3	Below Average
72	31	5	−1.9	3	Below Average
72	31.5	5	−1.85	3	Below Average
73	32	5	−1.8	4	Below Average
74	32.5	5	−1.75	4	Below Average
75	33	5	−1.7	5	Below Average
75	33.5	5	−1.65	5	Below Average
76	34	5	−1.6	5	Below Average
77	34.5	5	−1.55	6	Below Average
78	35	6	−1.5	7	Below Average
78	35.5	6	−1.45	7	Below Average
79	36	6	−1.4	8	Below Average
80	36.5	6	−1.35	9	Low Average
81	37	6	−1.3	10	Low Average
81	37.5	6	−1.25	10	Low Average
82	38	6	−1.2	12	Low Average
83	38.5	6	−1.15	13	Low Average
84	39	7	−1.1	14	Low Average
84	39.5	7	−1.05	14	Low Average
85	40	7	−1	16	Low Average
86	40.5	7	−0.95	18	Low Average
87	41	7	−0.9	19	Low Average
87	41.5	7	−0.85	19	Low Average
88	42	8	−0.8	21	Low Average

Standard Score	T Score	Scaled Score	Z Score	Percentile	Standard Descriptor
89	42.5	8	−0.75	23	Low Average
90	43	8	−0.7	25	Average
90	43.5	8	−0.65	25	Average
91	44	8	−0.6	27	Average
92	44.5	8	−0.55	30	Average
93	45	8	−0.5	32	Average
93	45.5	8	−0.45	32	Average
94	46	9	−0.4	34	Average
95	46.5	9	−0.35	37	Average
96	47	9	−0.3	39	Average
96	47.5	9	−0.25	39	Average
97	48	9	−0.2	42	Average
98	48.5	9	−0.15	45	Average
98	49	9	−0.1	45	Average
99	49.5	10	−0.05	47	Average
100	50	10	0	50	Average
101	50.5	10	0.05	53	Average
102	51	10	0.1	55	Average
102	51.5	10	0.15	55	Average
103	52	11	0.2	58	Average
104	52.5	11	0.25	61	Average
104	53	11	0.3	61	Average
105	53.5	11	0.35	63	Average
106	54	11	0.4	66	Average
107	54.5	11	0.45	68	Average
108	55	11	0.5	70	Average
108	55.5	12	0.55	70	Average
109	56	12	0.6	73	Average
110	56.5	12	0.65	75	High Average
111	57	12	0.7	77	High Average
111	57.5	12	0.75	77	High Average
112	58	12	0.8	79	High Average
113	58.5	13	0.85	81	High Average
114	59	13	0.9	82	High Average
114	59.5	13	0.95	82	High Average
115	60	13	1	84	High Average
116	60.5	13	1.05	86	High Average
117	61	13	1.1	87	High Average
117	61.5	13	1.15	87	High Average
118	62	14	1.2	88	High Average
119	62.5	14	1.25	90	High Average
120	63	14	1.3	91	Above Average
120	63.5	14	1.35	91	Above Average
121	64	14	1.4	92	Above Average
122	64.5	14	1.45	93	Above Average
123	65	14	1.5	94	Above Average
123	65.5	14	1.55	94	Above Average
124	66	15	1.6	95	Above Average
125	66.5	15	1.65	95	Above Average
126	67	15	1.7	96	Above Average
126	67.5	15	1.75	96	Above Average

Standard Score	*T Score*	*Scaled Score*	*Z Score*	*Percentile*	*Standard Descriptor*
127	68	15	1.8	96	Above Average
128	68.5	16	1.85	97	Above Average
129	69	16	1.9	97	Above Average
129	69.5	16	1.95	97	Above Average
130	70	16	2	98	Exceptionally High
131	70.5	16	2.05	98	Exceptionally High
132	71	16	2.1	98	Exceptionally High
132	71.5	16	2.15	98	Exceptionally High
133	72	17	2.2	99	Exceptionally High
134	72.5	17	2.25	99	Exceptionally High
135	73	17	2.3	99	Exceptionally High
135	73.5	17	2.35	99	Exceptionally High
136	74	17	2.4	99	Exceptionally High
137	74.5	17	2.45	99	Exceptionally High
138	75	17	2.5	99	Exceptionally High
138	75.5	17	2.55	99	Exceptionally High
139	76	18	2.6	99	Exceptionally High
140	76.5	18	2.65	99	Exceptionally High
141	77	18	2.7	99	Exceptionally High
141	77.5	18	2.75	99	Exceptionally High
142	78	18	2.8	99	Exceptionally High
143	78.5	18	2.85	99	Exceptionally High
144	79	19	2.9	99	Exceptionally High
144	79.5	19	2.95	99	Exceptionally High
145	80	19	3	99	Exceptionally High
146	80.5	19	3.05	99	Exceptionally High
147	81	19	3.1	99	Exceptionally High
147	81.5	19	3.15	99	Exceptionally High
148	82	20	3.2	99	Exceptionally High
149	82.5	20	3.25	99	Exceptionally High
150	83	20	3.3	99	Exceptionally High
150	83.5	20	3.35	99	Exceptionally High
151	84	20	3.4	99	Exceptionally High
152	84.5	20	3.45	99	Exceptionally High
153	85	20	3.5	99	Exceptionally High
153	85.5	20	3.55	99	Exceptionally High
154	86	20	3.6	99	Exceptionally High
155	86.5	20	3.65	99	Exceptionally High
155	87	20	3.7	99	Exceptionally High

Score Conversion: Quick Reference

Standard Score	*T Score*	*Scaled Score*	*Z Score*	*Percentile*	*Descriptor*
50	17	0	−3.33	<0.1	Exceptionally Low
55	20	1	−3	0.1	Exceptionally Low
60	23	2	−2.667	0.4	Exceptionally Low
65	27	3	−2.333	1	Exceptionally Low
70	30	4	−2	2	Below Average
75	33	5	−1.667	5	Below Average
80	37	6	−1.333	9	Low Average
85	40	7	−1	16	Low Average
90	43	8	−0.667	25	Average
93	45	8	−0.5	32	Average
95	47	9	−0.333	37	Average
100	50	10	0	50	Average
105	53	11	0.333	63	Average
108	55	11	0.5	70	Average
110	57	12	0.667	75	High Average
115	60	13	1	84	High Average
120	63	14	1.33	91	Above Average
125	67	15	1.667	95	Above Average
130	70	16	2	98	Exceptionally High
135	73	17	2.333	99	Exceptionally High
140	77	18	2.667	99	Exceptionally High
145	80	19	3	99	Exceptionally High
150	83	20	3.333	99	Exceptionally High

Standard Score	*T Score*	*Scaled Score*	*Z Score*	*Percentile*	*Descriptor*
40	10	0	−4	<1	Exceptionally Low
50	16.5		−3.5	<1	Exceptionally Low
55	20	1	−3	<1	Exceptionally Low
63	25		−2.5	1	Exceptionally Low
70	30	4	−2	2	Below Average
78	35		−1.5	7	Below Average
85	40	7	−1	16	Low Average
93	45		−0.5	32	Average
100	50	10	0	50	Average
108	55		.5	70	Average
115	60	13	1	84	High Average
123	65		1.5	94	Above Average
130	70	16	2	98	Exceptionally High
138	75		2.5	99	Exceptionally High

Score Table SAMPLE

Intellectual Ability

Test Name	Raw Score	Standard Score	Percentile	Descriptor
SCORE A				
SCORE B				
SCORE C				
Manual Reference (DATE)				

Attention/Executive Functioning

Test Name	Raw Score	Standard Score	Percentile	Descriptor
SCORE A				
SCORE B				
SCORE C				
Manual Reference (DATE)				

Language

Test Name	Raw Score	Standard Score	Percentile	Descriptor
SCORE A				
SCORE B				
SCORE C				
Manual Reference (DATE)				

Visual

Test Name	Raw Score	Standard Score	Percentile	Descriptor
SCORE A				
SCORE B				
SCORE C				
Manual Reference (DATE)				

Motor

Test Name	Raw Score	Standard Score	Percentile	Descriptor
SCORE A				
SCORE B				
SCORE C				
Manual Reference (DATE)				

Sensory

Test Name	Raw Score	Standard Score	Percentile	Descriptor
SCORE A				
SCORE B				
SCORE C				
Manual Reference (DATE)				

Verbal Memory

Test Name	Raw Score	Standard Score	Percentile	Descriptor
SCORE A				
SCORE B				
SCORE C				
Manual Reference (DATE)				

Visual Memory

Test Name	Raw Score	Standard Score	Percentile	Descriptor
SCORE A				
SCORE B				
SCORE C				
Manual Reference (DATE)				

Academics

Test Name	Raw Score	Standard Score	Percentile	Descriptor
SCORE A				
SCORE B				
SCORE C				
Manual Reference (DATE)				

Adaptive Functioning

Test Name	Raw Score	Standard Score	Percentile	Descriptor
SCORE A				
SCORE B				
SCORE C				
Manual Reference (DATE)				

Emotional and Behavioral Functioning

Test Name	Raw Score	Standard Score	Percentile	Descriptor
SCORE A				
SCORE B				
SCORE C				
Manual Reference (DATE)				

Personality Assessment

Test Name	Raw Score	Standard Score	Percentile	Descriptor
SCORE A				
SCORE B				
SCORE C				
Manual Reference (DATE)				

Symptom Validity Testing

Test Name	Raw Score	Standard Score	Percentile	Descriptor
SCORE A				
SCORE B				
SCORE C				
Manual Reference (DATE)				

Performance Validity Testing

Test Name	Raw Score	Standard Score	Percentile	Descriptor
SCORE A				
SCORE B				
SCORE C				
Manual Reference				

Psychometrist Competence and Skill Evaluation Form

Name of Psychometrist: ______________________
Name of Supervising Neuropsychologist: __________________
Date of Evaluation: ___/___/_____

Rating Scale

1 = Significantly below expected level of competence
2 = Below expected level of competence
3 = Competent/Satisfactory
4 = Above expected level of competence
5 = Significantly above expected level of competence
N/A = Not able to observe

Reflective Practice/Self-Assessment/Self-Care

- Acts in a professional, responsible and conscientious manner _____
- Dresses appropriately and demonstrates awareness of his/her direct reflection of the practice _____
- Arrives punctually and is timely in completing duties _____
- Demonstrates awareness of time management, appropriate resource allocation, and the importance of follow-through on tasks requested _____
- Accepts feedback in a non-defensive way and is responsive to supervisor suggestions _____
- Takes initiative, seeks consultation as needed, or looks for ongoing training opportunities. Willing to undertake broader system improvement projects _____
- Is self-reflective and able to discuss areas of competence, strengths/ weaknesses, and areas for growth _____
- OVERALL Reflective Practice/Self-Assessment/Self-Care rating _____

Comments:

Professional Identity **Rating**

- Assumes professional identity as psychometrist _____
- Acknowledges role differences across office personnel (e.g., psychometrist, neuropsychologist, office staff) and respects role boundaries _____
- Asserts oneself as a distinct professional on the team, taking responsibility for those expectations of the psychometrist and deferring to others when tasks are outside of one's bounds of competence _____
- Seeks opportunities to enhance professional development (e.g., training, didactics) _____
- OVERALL Professionalism rating _____

Comments:

Scientific Knowledge and Methods

• Maintains currency with key developments related to practice (e.g., new tests that are published, updates to current tests)	_____
• Demonstrates knowledge of behavioral observations across domains	_____
• Demonstrates understanding of standardized assessment practices	_____
• Demonstrates understanding of "testing the limits" and appropriate occasions for when it is used	_____
• Overall Scientific Knowledge & Methods Rating	_____

Comments:

Relationships: Interpersonal Skills and Communication	Rating
• Develops appropriate professional relationships with individuals in the workplace	_____
• Explains testing and the assessment process clearly and succinctly to clients or prospective clients	_____
• Listens attentively	_____
• Seeks clarification from others, as needed, to ensure accurate understanding	_____
• Respects and considers others' viewpoints and perspectives	_____
• Communicates verbally in an effective manner	_____
• Writes in an articulate and effective manner	_____
• Keeps call logs, forensic logs and other office protocols with meticulous attention to detail	_____
• Takes responsibility for mistakes/inappropriate behavior and takes action to correct situations swiftly, if they arise. Is also able to express awareness of how to handle the situation in the future	_____
• Manages difficult conversations in a clear, sensitive, and non-defensive manner	_____
• Respects others and is courteous in all interpersonal interactions	_____
• Articulates his/her own role in the evaluation process as well as expectations for testing to clients or family members in a clear, concise way	_____
• Establishes rapport with clients easily	_____
• OVERALL interpersonal skill/communication rating	_____

Comments:

Individual and Cultural Diversity	**Rating**
• Engages in ongoing professional development and training in order to enhance knowledge, recognize biases, and hone skills related to cultural diversity	_____
• Conveys comfort in interacting and working with diverse populations	_____
• Conveys respect for the differences of others, diverse values, ethical values, and world views	_____
• Recognizes personal biases and how individual differences can impact interactions with others	_____
• Seeks cultural consultation with others when misunderstandings/conflict arise regarding issues of diversity	_____
• OVERALL Diversity rating	_____

Comments:

Ethics, Legal Standards and Policy	**Rating**
• Demonstrates knowledge of the APA Ethics Code and other professional standards, guidelines, state statutes, rules, or other relevant regulations	_____
• Adheres to the APA Ethics Code in all professional endeavors, particularly those aspects that are pertinent to duties as a psychometrist	_____
• Recognizes ethical dilemmas as they arise and seeks supervision and consultation in a timely manner	_____
• Appreciates the importance of and adheres to highest standards of confidentiality, test security, and otherwise in the profession	_____
• Demonstrates sensitivity to ethical and legal considerations related to all professional activities	_____
• Practices appropriate professional assertiveness related to ethical issues (e.g., raising issues in a timely manner)	_____
• Seeks swift supervisory support when made aware of sensitive information (e.g., suicidality, child abuse, drug use)	_____
• OVERALL Ethics rating	_____

Comments:

Interdisciplinary Systems

- Demonstrates ability to communicate and interact knowledgeably with professionals across disciplines (e.g., neuropsychologists, school personnel, legal teams, front-office staff) _____
- Is able to work as a member of an interdisciplinary team and to collaborate with other professionals (e.g., neuropsychologist, office staff, trainees) _____
- OVERALL Interdisciplinary rating _____

Comments:

Assessment — Rating

- Arrives prepared to all assessment appointments, including protocols, materials, and so forth _____
- Organizes assessments to maximize efficiency with clients _____
- Establishes comfortable testing environment _____
- Administers assessments in a standardized manner adhering to professional procedures outlined in test manuals. _____
- Scores swiftly after administration, adhering to standardized scoring procedures _____
- Creates score table within 48 hours of client appointment date _____
- Checks for accuracy in administration, scoring, and other professional duties, and seeks consultation, as appropriate _____
- Stores and organizes test materials (manuals, protocols, manipulatives, etc.) in a clear and easily accessible manner _____
- Understands the importance of test security and protecting the integrity of test materials _____
- Records responses of the clients verbatim _____
- Maintains client records in an organized and efficient manner _____
- Makes keen behavioral observations and shares them with the neuropsychologist in a timely manner _____
- Scans file for long-term storage and shreds hard copy in a timely fashion _____
- Provides routine maintenance to testing supplies, as warranted _____
- OVERALL Assessment rating _____

Comments:

General Office/Admin Responsibilities	**Rating**
• Answers phones and responds to inquiries in a timely and professional manner	_____
• Responds to emails, letters, and other written communication in a timely and professional manner	_____
• Schedules patient appointments in a timely and professional manner	_____
• Places timely orders for supplies and maintains understanding of inventory of office materials	_____
• Responds promptly to requests for assistance by fellow office staff	_____
• Provides support for supplemental tasks, requested by the neuropsychologist	_____
• Corresponds with office maintenance teams (e.g., tech support, water supply, etc.) in timely fashion and keeps track of associated orders/invoices	_____
• Maintains documentation on the company shared drive in an organized and easily accessible manner	_____
• Maintains a tidy work environment	_____
• OVERALL General Office rating	_____

Comments:

I have had the opportunity to discuss this review with my supervisor.

Comments by psychometrist following review:

________________________ _____/_____/_________

Psychometrist Date of Review

________________________ _____/_____/_________

Neuropsychologist Supervisor Date of Review

Index

9780367564971